RESEARCHING YOUR PROFESSIONAL PRACTICE

DOING QUALITATIVE RESEARCH IN EDUCATIONAL SETTINGS

Series Editor: Pat Sikes

The aim of this series is to provide a range of high quality introductory research methods texts. Each volume focuses, critically, on one particular methodology enabling a detailed yet accessible discussion. All of the contributing authors are established researchers with substantial practical experience. While every book has its own unique style, each discusses the historical background of the approach, epistemological issues and appropriate uses. They then go on to describe the operationalization of the approach in educational settings drawing upon specific and vivid examples from the authors' own work. The intention is that readers should come away with a level of understanding that enables them to feel sufficiently confident to undertake their own research as well as to critically evaluate other accounts of research using the approach.

Published titles

Michael Bassey: *Case Study Research in Educational Settings*
Ivor Goodson and Pat Sikes: *Life History Research in Educational Settings*
Morwenna Griffiths: *Educational Research for Social Justice*
Gary McCulloch and William Richardson: *Historical Research in Educational Settings*
Jenny Ozga: *Policy Research in Educational Settings*
Hilary Radnor: *Researching Your Professional Practice*

RESEARCHING YOUR PROFESSIONAL PRACTICE

Doing interpretive research

Hilary Radnor

Open University Press
Buckingham · Philadelphia

Open University Press
Celtic Court
22 Ballmoor
Buckingham
MK18 1XW

email: enquiries@openup.co.uk
world wide web: www.openup.co.uk

and
325 Chestnut Street
Philadelphia, PA 19106, USA

First Published 2001

A catalogue record of this book is available from the British Library

ISBN 0 335 20764 2 (hb) 0 335 20763 4 (pb)

Library of Congress Cataloging-in-Publication Data
Radnor, Hilary A.
Researching your professional practice: doing interpretive research/Hilary Radnor.
p. cm. – (Doing qualitative research in educational settings)
Includes bibliographical references and index:
ISBN 0-335-20764-2 – ISBN 0-335-20763-4 (pbk.)
1. Education–Research. 2. Knowledge, Theory of. I. Title. II. Series.
LB1028.R242 2001
370′.7′2–dc21 2001032136

Typeset by Type Study, Scarborough
Printed in Great Britain by St Edmundsbury Press Ltd, Bury St Edmunds, Suffolk

Contents

Preface

This book is written to help all those researchers who wish to engage in research the interpretive way. It is particularly written for researchers who are also educational practitioners and are doing research for a further degree and/or to investigate professional practice. It provides a theoretical framework and demonstrates application of these theories to practices that have been honed through experience. What constitutes interpretive research is the explicit recognition of the researcher being engaged in the act of interpretation from the beginning of the research process to the end. My approach to research the interpretive way is driven by the belief that, at its best, interpretive educational research has explanatory power and can inspire through offering illuminating insights into human situations. In describing the process of interpretation Peshkin (2000: 9) concludes his paper on the nature of interpretation in qualitative research with the following statement, with which I wholeheartedly concur. 'To become forthcoming and honest about how we work as researchers is to develop a reflective awareness that, I believe, contributes to enhancing the quality of our interpretive acts.' Through making explicit my interpretive acts I sincerely hope this book will contribute to the enhancement of qualitative interpretive research practice.

The book is divided into three parts. Part 1 is entitled 'Understanding interpretive research' and is based on the assumption that it is not sufficient just to gain knowledge of a technique and to copy a method or follow a model of procedure to engage in interpretive research. It is necessary to understand the epistemological issues that make up this approach. In other words: what is it *to know* when we consider the social world and society, and when interacting with one another? The theoretical commitments and the philosophic assumptions that guide the approach of interpretive research advocated in this book are discussed in Chapter 1. Understanding the theory of interpretive research enables a deeper level of learning to take place. This encourages a critical perspective on the topic. However, in the first instance you might like to engage more directly with the researcher perspective and pragmatics of the approach, finding out what exactly you do before grappling with too much theory of method. If that is the case, then begin with Chapter 2. This focuses on my approach as an interpretive researcher, my distillation of the theories. Part 2 of the book, 'Undertaking interpretive research', follows on from this chapter and concentrates on how you should behave as an interpretive researcher. The final part of the book is entitled 'Describing interpretive research' and this consists of one chapter, which is a conversation between a PhD student and his supervisor. It is an opportunity to listen in on a dialogue about the student's practice that follows the interpretive principles explained in Part 2. Listening in on a conversation about process should help you link theory with practice and give you the chance to share a researcher's thought processes as he rationalizes his way towards the generation of an interpretation. Following reading Part 3 you might like to read Chapter 1, if you haven't done so already, so that you can engage with the theory that grounds the practice.

Writing about process can make the practice sound more complicated than it ought to be, so I have included examples of research practice to help to illuminate certain processes, as well as providing, in Part 2, a series of activities and exercises to enable you to practise some of the techniques.

I would like to acknowledge and sincerely thank five of my research students who have contributed to this book by providing research writings on different aspects of the interpretive process: Jean deRijke, Greta Grigoriou, James Hennessy, Amany Ahmed and Mamoom Al-Momeni. All these students' examples, I believe, give clarity to the approach and indicate to the reader the possibilities of this kind of research when you are a lone researcher with a very limited, or virtually non-existent, budget. What it takes is your time and intellectual effort. The other examples are taken from my own work and much of that is in collaboration with other interpretive researchers: particular thanks go to Stephen Ball and Malcolm Ross. These projects are well referenced in the text.

I would also like to thank all the research students who have attended my methodology sessions, where the ideas in this book have been developed. Their interest and comments have helped me, as a writer about research, to demystify the process in such a way that new researchers can engage in the exciting process of researching their own and others' professional practice.

Finally, I should like to dedicate this book to Mariella and Samuel, for whom life is but one long adventure and who I expect will be exploring and researching their world well into the twenty-first century.

Part 1 | Understanding interpretive research

Chapter 1 discusses the theoretical commitments and the philosophical assumptions that guide the approach of interpretive research in educational settings. A detailed commentary on the concept of interpretation and the roots of interpretive research is presented. The theory covered in Chapter 1 forms the basis from which the author as researcher takes her approach to doing research. Chapter 2 presents the author's view of social reality and her approach to knowledge, which underpins the methodology which makes up the rest of the book. The author's commentary on the approach can be understood without reading Chapter 1 but reading Chapter 1 will deepen the reader's understanding of the stance she is taking. However, it is perfectly possible to save the reading of Chapter 1 until you have read Part 2.

1 | A perspective on interpretive research

Education deals in knowledge. Knowledge is both the subject and the object of the enterprise. The professional educator is a knowledge worker in two fundamental ways. The content of the work engaged in is knowledge, and in order to engage in the work of enabling others to learn, the practitioner has to know how the process of knowing works. Theories of how we know, i.e. theories of cognition, have advanced the notion that, as Resnick (1991: 1) puts it:

> the empiricist assumption that dominated many branches of psychology for decades, the assumption that what we know is a direct reflection of what we can perceive in the physical world has largely disappeared. In its place is a view that most knowledge is an interpretation of experience.

We interpret experiences through the filters of existing knowledge and beliefs, and these existing knowledge and beliefs that we hold are a product of ourselves as active subjects construing meaning.

> The earlier dominant philosophical view of mind, learning and knowledge was 'egocentric' focusing on the individual and how one acquired true knowledge of the world external to oneself. The newer view is 'sociocentric', still considering the individual and the world but taking into account the cultural nature of knowledge as a communal human construction that is both formed by and forms human beings.
>
> (Soltis 1981: 97)

So individuals construct personal meanings in the context of the ideas, thoughts and beliefs and values provided by the social and cultural environment in which they live and these ideas, thoughts, beliefs and values can only be made meaningful to individuals to the extent that they make sense of them.

Education is a field of study within the social sciences. Professionals in the educational system construct personal meanings when they grapple with interpreting the social world of educational policy and making meaningful the implementation of that policy in the working practices of schools and in classrooms.

The interpretive approach rests on the premise that in social life there is only interpretation. Everyday life revolves around persons interpreting and making decisions about how to act based on their own experiences and their interpretation of the experience and behaviour of others. The purpose of interpretive research is to clarify how interpretations and understandings are formulated, implemented and given meaning in lived situations. 'The interpretation aims to bring to light an underlying coherence or sense' (Taylor 1995: 15). The process of clarification illuminates the everyday theories people have that inform their conduct and their experiences, and hence the value of the research enterprise is to help with this process through broadening the practitioner's knowledge base and to aid a deeper understanding of both action and context. It should inform practitioners' activities as knowledge workers and help them to help others to learn in a highly structured and complex education system.

What is interpretivism?

Interpretivists argue for the uniqueness of human inquiry, and to understand human action by means of interpretation is to argue for an altogether different aim from natural science. Erickson (1990: 98) explains this shift as follows:

> If people take action on the grounds of their interpretation of the actions of others, then meaning interpretations themselves are causal for humans. This is not true in nature . . . The billiard ball does not make sense of its environment. But the human actor in society does and different humans make sense differently. They impute symbolic meaning to others' actions and take their own actions in accord with the meaning interpretations they have made.

It is worth noting that different interpretive researchers would prioritize different scholars and thinkers in providing an explanation of interpretivism. However, my blend of interpretivism intermingles the social theory of action and ideas from the intellectual tradition of hermeneutics about the nature of understanding, which impacts on the *Verstehen* position of sociology and the role of language as a medium of practical social activity. These dimensions of interpretivism will now be discussed in turn.

The social theory of action

The social theory of action emphasizes that social actors make social life and that the actor is able to be creative in doing so. Action theories have a view of society that emphasizes the connection between action and meanings. Society (or aspects of society, such as institutions) as such does not act, only people do that. What is done, who does it and why matter to people – social actors – when they decide on what they do and how they respond to others. When looked at from this point of view, meaning and understanding are the stuff of social life, they constitute it.

The name associated with the origination of the social action theory – the action frame of reference – is Max Weber (1864–1920). He defined social action thus:

> Sociology . . . is a science which attempts the interpretive understanding of social action. In 'action' is included all human behaviour when and in so far as the acting individual attaches a subjective meaning to it. Action in this sense may be either overt or purely inward or subjective; it may consist of positive intervention in a situation, or of deliberately refraining from such intervention or passively acquiescing in the situation. Action is social in so far as, by virtue of the subjective meaning attached to it by the acting individual (or individuals) it takes account of the behaviour of others and is thereby oriented in its course.
> (Weber 1964: 88)

He stated that in order to explain an action we must be attentive to the meanings of others' lives, to the 'deciphering' of the inner meanings of social phenomena. This understanding of the subjective intended meaning is termed *Verstehen*. The notion of *Verstehen* was central to Weber's sociology. He claimed that the ultimate goal was to analyse the individual person, believing that the individual was the sole carrier of meaningful conduct. The sociology of social action was further developed by two influential thinkers linked to two particular interpretive perspectives, George Herbert Mead and his theory of symbolic interactionism and Alfred Schutz and his sociological perspective on phenomenology.

Symbolic interactionism

Weber's views stressing the meaningful purposive nature of human action has affinities with the analysis of human action processes asserted by the social psychologist George Herbert Mead (1863–1931). He developed the notion of *Verstehen* as an image of the individual and society that is interactional. He interplays individual and society through the process of communication. Blumer (1971: 11) writes of Mead's depiction of human society:

> His treatment took the form of showing that human group life was the essential condition of the emergence of consciousness, the mind,

a world of objects, human beings as organisms possessing selves and human conduct in the form of constructed acts.

The central tenets of Mead that influenced sociology and gave rise to a perspective called symbolic interactionism can be summarized under the following headings:

- the reflexive self;
- the human ability to take on 'the role of the other';
- the notion of social action as process;
- language as the predominant symbol of communication.

In *Mind, Self and Society*, Mead explains his concept of self as:

> something which has developed; it is not initially there at birth but arises in the process of social experience and activity, that is, develops in the given individual as a result of his relations to that process as a whole and to the other individuals within that process.
> (Mead 1934: 144)

He sees self as reflexive, the human as a self-conscious being. The individual is only able to experience himself or herself through seeing himself or herself as others do. This seeing ourselves as others see us is defined by Mead as 'taking on the role of the other'. And it allows the individual to define his or her situation and choose his or her own actions. Taking on the role of the other is developed through the individual's ability to communicate both with himself or herself and with others. So being self-conscious in the Meadian sense is to be conscious of one's self as object. This allows us to talk to ourselves as self-conscious individuals in the social context.

> The individual experiences himself as such, not directly but only indirectly, from the particular standpoints of other individual members of the same social group or from the generalised standpoint of the social group as a whole to which he belongs. For he enters his own experience as a self or individual, not directly or immediately, not by becoming a subject to himself, but only in so far as he first becomes an object to himself just as other individuals are objects to him or are in his experience; and he becomes an object to himself only by taking the attitudes of other individuals towards himself within a social environment or context of experience and behaviour in which he and they are involved.
> (Mead 1934: 146)

This development of self arises out of the process of communication. Self and other awareness is constructed and created as we grow up from a child to an adult. As children, in a social environment we operate in a world that is full of symbols that are carried in language. We learn to interpret these symbols and in acquiring this knowledge are able to use it for our own purposes and to reflect on it. We are empowered to share and understand this symbolic representation of the world through the interactive nature of self and others. This ability to reflect on ourselves and to see ourselves as others see us means we are able to anticipate the responses of others to us.

> The self as that which can be object to itself, is essentially a social structure and it arises out of social experience . . . It is impossible to conceive of a self arising outside of social experience. That process . . . of responding to one's self as another responds to it, taking part in one's own conversation with others, being aware of what one is saying and using that awareness of what one is saying to determine what one is going to say thereafter – that is a process of which we are familiar. We are continually following up our own address to other persons by an understanding of what we are saying and using that understanding in the direction of our continued speech. We are finding out what we are going to say, what we are going to do, by saying and doing and in the process we are continually controlling the process itself.
>
> (Mead 1934: 147)

Mead maintains that the human individual is only able to develop a self in the fullest sense by not only taking the attitude of others towards himself or herself but also taking the attitude of the community or the social group, which he terms 'the generalised other'.

> It is in the form of the generalised other that the social process influences the behaviour of the individuals involved in it and carrying it on, that is, that the community exercises control over the conduct of its individual members; for it is in this form that the social process or community enters as a determining factor in the individual's thinking. In abstract thought the individual takes the attitude of the generalised other towards himself without reference to its expression in any particular other individual; and in concrete thought, he takes that attitude in so far as it is expressed in the attitudes towards his behaviour of those individuals with whom he is involved in the given social situation or act. But only by taking the attitude of the generalised other toward himself, in one or another of these ways, can he think at all; for only thus can thinking – or the internalised conversation of gestures which constitutes thinking – occur. And only through the taking by individuals of the attitude or attitudes of the generalised other towards themselves is the existence of a universe of discourse, as that system of common or social meanings which thinking presupposes as its context, rendered possible.
>
> (Mead 1934: 150)

What Mead is telling us here is that the self is an individual who is a social object to himself or herself. To be a social object to oneself means that the individual acquires meanings similar to the meanings held by those around one through the interactive symbolic communication process of interpretation. In this way the individual is in society and the society is in the individual. But because the individual is able to think and reflect she or he is also able to create and construct new meanings, building on the old meanings. In this sense individuals, collectives of individuals, institutions and societies themselves are open to change. The continuity and novelty, the stability and change of our private lives means that we are not only controlled by the society that precedes us but we are also empowered to change it. Mead (1934: 89) writes:

> This view . . . frees us from the bondage either to past or future. We are neither creatures of necessity or of an irrevocable past, nor of any vision given on the mount. Our values lie in the present, and past and future give us only a schedule of means, and the plans of campaign, for their realisation.

In the philosophy of G. H. Mead we are in some ways creators of both ourselves and our society. We are active participants in the world, and through the complex interactive processes that he analyses, our self-identity as social beings, the meanings that we ascribe to our own and others social situations and acts and the roles we take on in acting out our lives, our lives are created, perpetuated, adapted and transformed. The constant interplay of personal, social and structural features all influence social situations. Thus, as Rock (1979) points out:

> The symbolic interactionists reject subjective idealism because they acknowledge the stubborn facticity of the world, yet they also resist the gross empiricism which depicts objects and relations as laden with innative meaning.
>
> (cited in Meighan 1981: 230)

The interactionist vision of people in society is one of active agents participating in a dynamic changing network of interaction framed within structural conditions. As Herbert Blumer, an exponent of symbolic interactionism, states:

> People – that is acting units – do not act towards culture, social structures or the like; they act towards situations. Social organisation enters into the action only to the extent to which it supplies fixed sets of symbols which people use in interpreting their situation.
>
> (Blumer 1962: 190)

Sociological phenomenology

Phenomenologists describe and interpret the phenomena of personal lived experiences, their own and/or other people's. The interest is in the contextualized personal individual meanings, with the aim of understanding and recording the meanings which people make of their experiences.

Alfred Schutz (1899–1959) developed a form of phenomenology called sociological phenomenology, in which he problematized the assumptions embedded in the Weberian conceptualization of *Verstehen*. Schutz focused his analysis on the notion of intersubjectivity, which Weber failed to elucidate. People draw on a shared set of social concepts, symbols and meanings. Whereas symbolic interactionism shows how shared definitions are built up through communication in interaction, Schutz's thesis is that individuals share a stock of common knowledge of taken for granted assumptions about society, other actors and the world. The basic structure of the social world rests upon acts of establishing or interpreting meaning, and while interacting with each other people assume a reciprocity of perspectives, an idea that is very close to Mead's 'taking on the role of the other'.

The central tenets of Schutz that have influenced sociologists can be summarized under the following headings:

- intersubjectivity;
- common-sense knowledge;
- clarification of *Verstehen*;
- a particular methodology for social science.

Schutz had a view of sociology as a discipline whose prime aim was to obtain organized knowledge of social reality. Writing in the *Journal of Philosophy* (1954), from which all the quotes in this section are taken, he defined social reality as:

> The sum total of objects and occurrences within the social cultural world as experienced by the common-sense thinking of men living their daily lives among their fellow-men, connected with them in manifold relations of interaction. It is a world of cultural objects and social institutions into which we are born, within which we have to find our bearings and with which we have to come to terms.

Through intercommunication and language, this world is not a private world but an intersubjective one. It presents itself to the individual in the form of an objectified system which each individual takes for granted. So although the everyday social world is experienced through the individual consciousness, it is not experienced as 'private' to each individual, but as a common shared world in which the individual is involved.

> Common-sense knowledge of everyday life is sufficient for coming to terms with fellow-men, cultural objects, social institutions – in brief social reality. This is so because the world is from the outset an intersubjective world and because our knowledge of it is in various ways socialised. Moreover the social world is experienced from the outset as a meaningful one. The Other's body is not experienced as an organism but as a fellow-man, its overt behaviour not as an occurrence in the

> space-time of the outer world, but as our fellow-man's action. We normally 'know' what the Other does, for what reason he does it, why he does it at that particular time and in these circumstances.

This common-sense thinking about the world leads the social actor to experience the shared world as the world 'out there' and his or her personal involvement in it as the subjective aspect – the particularities of the individual within common-shared meanings. Given this approach to social action, Schutz clarified *Verstehen* as not so much about introspection but more about grasping the intersubjective meanings and symbolizing activities that constitute social life. '*Verstehen* is, thus, primarily not a method used by the social scientist but the particular existential form in which common-sense thinking takes cognisance of the social cultural world.' He believed that Weber termed it subjective because it was about finding out what the actor means in his action rather than what the observer thinks the actor means by observing him. Schutz makes a case for the differences between the subjective individual and the intersubjective social world that is perceived by the individual as objective by stating that the common-sense knowledges shared by members of the society are 'typifications'.

> The world of everyday is from the outset a social cultural world in which I am interrelated in manifold ways of interaction with fellow-men known to me in varying degrees of intimacy and anonymity. To a certain extent, sufficient for many practical purposes I understand their behaviour if I understand their motives and goals, choices and plans originated in their biographically determined circumstances. Yet only in particular situations and then only fragmentarily can I experience the others' motives, goals, etc. – briefly the subjective meanings they bestow upon their actions in their uniqueness. I can, however, experience them in typicality.

The more interconnected patterns of behaviour, such as those socially approved via laws, practices, custom etc., can be said to be *typical* of what happens in that society, then the more they have utility when it comes to interpreting human action in the social world. The features of the constructs of the common-sense experience of everyday life (which is fundamentally intersubjective) have implications for social science methodology. The observations made by the social scientist have to take into account the fact that social reality has a meaning and relevance for the human beings living within it.

> By a series of common-sense constructs they have pre-selected and pre-interpreted this world which they experience as the reality of their daily lives. It is these thought objects of theirs which determine their behaviour by motivating it. The thought objects constructed by the social scientists, in order to grasp this social reality, have to be founded upon

> the thought objects constructed by the common-sense thinking of men, living their daily life within their social world. Thus, the constructs of the social sciences are, so to speak, constructs of the second degree, that is, constructs of the constructs made by the actors on the social scene, whose behaviour the social scientist has to observe and to explain in accordance with the procedural rules of science.

The social construction of reality

The sociological approach articulated by Weber and Schutz and the symbolic interactionist perspective are (re) interpreted in the Berger and Luckman text entitled *The Social Construction of Reality*, first published in the UK in 1966. This work is a systematic theoretical treatise on the sociology of knowledge. It is an analysis of knowledge in everyday life that generates a theory of society as a dialectical process between objective and subjective reality which encapsulates succinctly the general thesis of the social action theorists.

> It is important to emphasise that in the relationship between man, the producer and the social world, his product is and remains a dialectical one. That is man (not, of course in isolation but in his collectivities) and his social world interact with each other. The product acts back upon the producer. Externalization and objectivation are moments in a continuing dialectical process. The third moment in this process, which is internalization (by which the objectivated social world is retrojected into consciousness in the course of socialization) will occupy us in considerable detail later on. It is already possible, however, to see the fundamental relationship of these three dialectical moments in social reality. Each of them correspond to an essential characterization of the social world. *Society is a human product. Society is an objective reality. Man is a social product.*
>
> (Berger and Luckman 1966: 78)

The world of the first person subject is prioritized but, within the research practice, the researcher disengages from that experience and objectifies it in a similar way to the notion of objectivation articulated above. The belief system expounded by Weber, Schutz and the symbolic interactionists states that methodologically human sciences are different to the natural sciences and so need a different approach to method. Weber (1947: 98–9) comes up with a conception of adequacy on the level of meaning; a conceptual framework of analysis of ideal types is used to interpret social phenomena. Schutz, in responding to the question of how it is possible to form objective concepts and an objective verifiable theory of subjective meaning-constructs, cites Weber and his school of thought. Blumer (1962) (following Mead) perceives sociological concepts such as definition of the situation, status, role, belief and so on as 'sensitizing concepts' rather than as variables to be measured. The sensitizing concepts act as a theoretical framework that explains social phenomena.

However, there are philosophical ideas that take us beyond this subject/object debate by accepting fully the hermeneutic character of existence, and it is to this school of thought that we now turn.

The intellectual tradition of hermeneutics

The philosophical hermeneutics of Heidegger, Gadamar and Taylor discussed in this section makes claims that the activity of interpretation is the very nature of inquiry itself. As Rabinow and Sullivan (1987: 20) state, 'The interpretive turn is not simply a new methodology, but rather a challenge to the very idea that inquiry into the social world and the value of understanding that results is to be determined by methodology.'

The intellectual tradition of hermeneutics brings to the interpretivist approach key ideas about the nature of understanding and the role of language as a medium of practical social activity, because conceiving the activity of interpretation in terms of ontology impacts on the relationship between the researcher and the researched. As Rabinow and Sullivan (1987: 6) put it, 'For the human sciences both the object of investigation – the web of language, symbol and institution – and the tools by which the investigation is carried out share inescapably the same persuasive context that is the human world.'

The hermeneutic interpretation of understanding

The philosopher Martin Heidegger (1889–1976) presented a radical new meaning to the study of the phenomenon of understanding. He stated that understanding is an ontological condition, not an epistemological one. In other words, understanding is a mode of being rather than a mode of knowledge. To be is to understand: understanding has to be grasped as an essence of existence.

Whereas up to the time of Heidegger the problem of hermeneutics was concerned with discovering the correct interpretation of what has been understood, Heidegger asked not what is to be done to obtain correct understanding but, as Bauman (1978: 148) describes it, 'What in the human mode of being-in-the-world, determines both the possibility and the actuality of understanding?'

In the first instance it is necessary to make sense of Heidegger's notion of 'being-in-the-world' in order to grasp his perspective on understanding and the impact it has had on interpretive sociology. As Gadamer (1989: 259), in discussing Heidegger's perspective, states, 'Understanding . . . is the original form of the realization of *Dasein*, which is being-in-the-world.'

Dasein is Heidegger's conception of what it is to be human. To be in the world of *Dasein* is not the same as one object being in another, like sweets in a jar or beer in a can. It is more about the structure of one's existence as opposed to an object in space. This structure of existence is a state of continuous being, the duality between subject and object is extinguished. There is no need to prove the existence of an external world. Gelven (1970: 126, 128) in his commentary on Heidegger states that:

> to prove the existence of an external world is to overlook the apriori nature of being-in-the-world . . . Rocks and trees do not depend on man for their occurrence in the universe, but reality, which is merely a mode of man's interpretation of the world, does depend on man's existence.

According to Heidegger, the *Dasein* – the existence typical of humans – takes reality for granted. All is there in existence naturally and unproblematically. My existence and the world of my existence are one, 'given-to-hand' as Heidegger expresses it. What this means is that when all is in perfect harmony the human being does not distinguish between his or her existence and the world of his or her existence. However, this perfect harmony is not always the nature of the human's existence. As Bauman (1978: 159) puts it:

> if the world functioned smoothly and without interruption, if there was perfect harmony between my hand stretched towards the world and the shape of the world the hand is stretched to handle, if the two were perfectly geared to each other. But there is no such harmony. The hand stretched towards the world is likely to hang in the void, or touch a rugged surface or catch an object too large or unwieldy to be grasped. The world is fraught with such incongruities.

When this happens the process of theoretical knowledge is triggered off. The given-to-hand is no longer taken for granted. The given-to-hand becomes a thing out there, an object waiting for our theoretical knowledge to give it qualities. We see things as objects, when they don't fit our actuality, when the object has other possibilities. It becomes a thing separate from ourselves that has to be separately conceived, conceptualized. Bauman again: 'In so far as our world is human, the lack of identity between possibility and actuality and therefore theoretical knowledge is not just conceived, but inevitable' (p. 160).

Understanding begins when something addresses us. We question. The essence of a question opens up possibilities. Knowing things theoretically means that we distance ourselves from ourselves and look at ourselves as objects. We lift ourselves from ourselves from the mode of just 'being there' to the mode of understanding. Understanding begins when a gap opens between the way I am already and the realm of my possibilities. As Gadamer (1989: 260) puts it, 'Understanding is the original characteristic of the being of human life itself . . . Thus it is true in every case that a person who understands, understands himself, projecting himself upon his possibilities.'

The sociological implication of perceiving understanding as an ontological condition is in the recognition that we are a product of our history. And because we are a product of our history, understanding is always an understanding of history: past and present are being constantly mediated. *Verstehen* is therefore not simply a special method of the social science of understanding, but is the nature of the existence of human society as it is produced and reproduced by its members. Understanding derives its actuality from the historical totality in which it is immersed. Gadamer uses the term tradition. Our understanding can only be within the tradition in which we find ourselves; it is not so much a subjective act as a participation in an event of tradition. To put it another way, the interpretive researcher recognizes that as the social world is a historical one, we live in history, we create history. We do not live in a human social world that is biologically programmed. It is the performance of members of society that produce and reproduce it. As Giddens (1993: 168) states, 'Society is not concerned with a pre-given universe of objects but with one which is constituted or produced by the active doing of subjects.'

The role of language

We are caught up in the hermeneutic circle. Gadamer, following Heidegger, describes the circular movement of understanding as being neither subjective nor objective but the interplay of the movement of tradition and the movement of the interpreter. Understanding, for example, a text or a culture different from our own, or the action of 'others', means entering into a conversation, a discourse through seeking for shared meanings – meanings that are produced and reproduced in the movement of history, frames of meanings that predate each of us as individuals.

In order to understand we have to learn the language of our society. To take part in conversation or discourse helps us to make sense of our society. To be able to communicate with others means we share a form of life. We recognize what it is to be human. Language is the universal medium in which understanding occurs. Understanding occurs in interpreting. Gadamer (1976: 115) puts it thus:

> Thought is dependent upon the ground of language in so far as language is not merely a system of signs for the purpose of communication and transmission of information . . . Rather within our language

> relationship to the world, that which is spoken of is itself first articulated through language's constitutive structuring of our being in the world.

This theme of the intertwining of thought and language, being as manifest in language (Gadamer, 1989), is a fundamental theme of the writings of Wittgenstein (1889–1951). Wittgenstein did not first and foremost see language as a system of signs and representations, but as an expression of the human mode of 'being in the world'. Wittgenstein drew our attention to the situated condition of language, to the context of words as enabling us to communicate. We understand what people say to us, not because we grasp a link between the words and the speaker's intention, getting into her 'mental processes', but because we 'know' the language, we engage in a communicative act. When we communicate with one another in the same language, what matters is that we use concepts in the same way, not that our private experience of the meaning of concepts differ. In discussing Wittgenstein, Bauman (1978: 214) gives an example to clarify this point.

> When I ask you to give me a red pencil, I can reasonably expect you to give me one. Yet I have no idea how you experience the 'redness' of the pencil; whether your experience of redness is 'like' mine. The point is, however, that this knowledge is unnecessary for our interaction to take place to mutual satisfaction. We both know how to go on in spite of the fact that both of us have only our private, uncommunicable experiences of redness. The only thing which really matters is that both you and me use the word 'red' in the same way, i.e. we both use it as a name for the same set of objects . . . The 'sameness' of your and my usage of the word 'red' is grounded in our knowledge of language and not in the 'sameness' of our experience of redness.

Through language the meanings of things are arrived at referentially and relationally. The philosopher Charles Taylor (1995), in discussing the nature of interpretation, makes the case of the sameness of our use of words in the same way, as being common meanings that define our social reality. So, although it may well be that social reality exists independently of the vocabulary of society, it cannot in fact be identified separate from the language used to describe it.

> The range of human desires, feelings, emotions, and hence meanings is bound up with the level and type of culture, which in turn is inseparable from the distinctions and categories marked by the language people speak. The field of meanings in which the given situation can find its place is bound up with the semantic field of the terms characterising these meanings and the related feelings, desires and predicaments . . . The situation we have here is one in which the vocabulary of a given social dimension is grounded in the shape of social practice in

> this dimension; that is the vocabulary would not make sense, could not be applied sensibly, where this range of practices did not prevail. And yet this range of practices could not exist without the prevalence of this or that related vocabulary. There is no simple one-way dependence here. We can speak of mutual dependence if we like, but really what this points up is the artificiality of the distinction between social reality and the language of description of the social reality. The language is constitutive of the reality, is essential to its being the kind of reality it is.
>
> (Taylor 1995: 25, 33)

The sociological implications of this perspective on language lead to the recognition that we only know what we think and mean. We cannot know what others think and mean in the same sense that we know ourselves. We can only know others through their actions and the words they speak. When we talk about understanding others at the level of meaning we are referring to our interpretation of what we see and hear. But as we share a form of life, through our language we are capable of reconstructing experiences other than our own. We engage in dialogic acts with others, an interpretive process through which comes further new understandings.

Concluding thoughts

Taking an interpretive stance towards the social world, or rather within social life (because we are part of it and not able to stand outside it), deepens one's sense of the basic interpretability of life itself.

> This is a matter of taking up the interpretive task for oneself rather than simply receiving the delivered goods as bearing the final word. This sounds trivial, perhaps, but we live in a world with many 'heavy' interpretations: ideologies and fundamentalisms masquerade as forms of truth lying beyond the reach of interpretation itself. Indeed in a time when the very act of thinking has become a target of intense commercial and political manipulation, the need is great for persons who can meaningfully deconstruct what is going on and propose alternative, more creative ways of thinking and acting.
>
> (Smith 1991: 199)

2 | Personal approach to interpretivism

Chapter 1 offered a perspective on interpretivism drawing from philosophers and sociologists whose ideas about the nature of being in the world (ontological considerations) and the nature of knowledge (epistemology) have been influential in generating the frames of meaning (Giddens's term) or the paradigm (Kuhn's term) within which the interpretive approach is situated. This chapter offers the reader insight into my theoretical approach within interpretivism, which informs me as an educational researcher and justifies my research methodology principles and consequent research practices that make up the rest of the book.

My theoretical approach to researching education

The basis of where I am coming from as an interpretive researcher is coming to grips with the social world, which is fundamentally different from the natural world because in the social world, people have their own intentions, their feelings and emotions, impacted by each other as well as the context in which they live. Education is part of my social world and the education system is an organized entity within the structure of society.

In terms of researching aspects of the education system, it could be approached, theoretically, either from the perspective of the actions of individuals within the educational arena or from perceiving the education system in structural terms and basing the research on, for example, structural functionalist notions. Functionalism depicts society as essentially integrated and cohesive, with a common set of norms and values that lead to consensus. So, with respect to the education system the task of researching educational issues would look at the way the structural arrangements influence the behaviour of the participants in the system, and would be concerned about the maintenance of order. There is the underlying belief in the importance of the education system as part of one element of the interrelated nature of society that needs to perform effectively in order for society to retain an equilibrium. An influential sociological thinker in the development of functionalism, Emile Durkeim (1858–1917), in a lecture delivered in 1902 defined 'true education' as being a certain number of ideas, attitudes and practices that everyone should have. He said: 'not only is it society which has raised the human type to the dignity of a model that the educator must attempt to reproduce, but it is society, too, that builds this model, and it builds it according to its needs' (Durkheim 1956: 122).

So, from a functionalist perspective, schooling contributes to the cohesion of society, by transmitting to new generations the central or 'core' values of that society. One could argue that our government has a functionalist perspective on schooling, with the concept of a national curriculum delivered to all pupils regardless of their background, interests, ethnic origin etc. A national curriculum has the effect of transmitting the same knowledge across a wide spectrum of society. The school, therefore, through implementing a national curriculum, promotes a consensus about the basic knowledge and values necessary for children to have in our society. A researcher in this perspective would perceive the breakdown of order or issues of dissent as resulting in dysfunctional behaviour, and would research how this could be rectified so that equilibrium could be resumed. The emphasis in this approach is the society as an entity, external to and 'bigger' than the individuals that make it up, and taking precedence over the needs of the individual. It is as if, as individuals in society, we 'learn how to function', we follow a 'script' of reasoned behaviour so that our behaviour is fairly predictable.

The problem I have with a structural functionalist perspective is the emphasis on the view of society as a solid entity, and the education system as reified, existing outside of those individuals that make it up, as socially and culturally defined in a set of rules that we have to follow. It paints a picture of conformist actors in a deterministic social world, living within constraints. Structural conditions clearly impact on individual actions, but it is the activities of human beings that produce society and also, therefore, the social systems that make it up. We are living in a time of constant change, change generated by individuals who make up the structures and systems that inhabit our world. It seems to me that an approach to the study of social structures that perceives human beings as simply enacting imposed cultural rules does not help us to understand the processes of intense social change that have become the norm in society. Education has become a central feature of societal change, dealing as it does with knowledge and the development of skills.

> For the first time in history, knowledge is the primary source of economic productivity. It has begun to penetrate most of the products that we create, and become a core resource for organisations and an emblem of individual employability. Technological progress, organisational

> change and intensified global competition have driven a shift from manual work to 'thinking' jobs that emphasise a whole new range of skills, from problem-solving and communication to information and risk management and self-organisation.
>
> (Seltzer and Bentley 1999: 9)

Proactive, creative individuals are not only altering our perceptions of society but also transforming the structures that make up our social worlds. A research approach that centrally incorporates the notion of the creative subject at the heart of social life is imperative to an understanding of the forces of development and change. In educational research, the perspective of interactionism recognizes the existence of structural conditions and, within these conditions, the way that people interpret the meaning of the process and practices as they appear to them in the situations that confront them and how they construct new forms of action as a result of that interpretation. The individual is at the forefront, interacting, negotiating and having influence on the groups and the organizations of which she or he is a part. Hargreaves (1972) gives a clear account of the relationship between people and the structures within which they act. He states that the impact of definitions and meanings on the social structure of human action is clearly expressed in the phrase 'the definition of the situation', which was coined by W. I. Thomas. Hargreaves writes:

> What sociologists call culture can be seen as a set of collective definitions. Thomas emphasised that these collective definitions are not fully shared . . . in spite of such contradictions that are evident within cultures, social interactions can proceed only when to a large degree the participants have a common definition of the situation . . . Some elements of the definition of the situation are given, and come to constitute the agreed and taken for granted overall definition of the situation. Other elements are unique to the individual participant, who has his own version of the definition of the situation . . . We take the overall definition of the situation for granted because it does not have to be negotiated de novo every time. But this should not blind us to the process of progressive negotiation and modification that has taken place.
>
> (Hargreaves 1972: 104–6)

The interactionist perspective of the active creative resonates with Giddens's (1984: 3, 21–2) perspective on the human being as a purposive agent:

> To be a human being is to be a purposive agent who both has reasons for his or her activities and is able, if asked, to elaborate discursively upon the reasons . . . Awareness of social rules, expressed first and foremost in practical consciousness, is the very core of that 'knowledgeability' which specifically characterises human agents. As social actors, all human beings are highly 'learned' in respect of knowledge which

> they possess, and apply, in the production and reproduction of day-to-day social encounters.

The subject/agent exists within a social context. Therefore, it is necessary for me as researcher to grapple with the relationship between the valuing, meaning-attributing human and the societal structures that humans create, i.e. the institutions, systems, laws and organizations which we inhabit and which inhabit our world. Giddens theorizes the relationship between agency and structure, calling the theory 'structuration'. He uses the term structuration to synthesize the two elements: people as active forces in social systems and people working within structured situations. He describes it as a dialectical relationship, a complex interplay between the constraints of structures and agent's autonomy – a double involvement of interdependence in which human beings create society and are at the same time created by it.

This vision of people in society as one of the active agents participating in a dynamic changing network of interaction framed within structural conditions is one that I ascribe to and is my theoretical approach to interpretivism. The following extract from Beck (1979: 12) captures the spirit in which I work.

> The purpose of social science is to understand social reality as different people see it and to demonstrate how their views shape the action which they take within that reality. Since the social sciences cannot penetrate to what lies behind social reality, they must work directly with man's definitions of reality and with the rules he devises for coping with it. While the social sciences do not reveal ultimate truth, they do help us to make sense of our worlds. What the social sciences offer is explanation, clarification and demystification of the social forms which man has created around himself.

Epistemological implications

The research commitment is therefore to come to grips with the social world which people inhabit. To render these worlds intelligible, the focus is upon the social construction of reality and the ways in which social interaction reflects actors' unfolding definitions of their situations. As Hughes (1976: 25) puts it, 'Human beings are not things to be studied in the way one studies rats, plants or rocks, but as valuing meaning-attributing beings to be understood as subjects and known as subjects.' Human beings as valuing, meaning-attributing beings, the notion of *Verstehen*, is the fundamental epistemological principle that guides my work. Knowledge is only possible through the interpretive processes which I, as researcher, enact in my encounters with the subjects of my inquiry. As a subject myself, I do not see my attributes and behaviour as external to myself, and by that I mean I can only 'come to know' through my subjective understanding. I can never get to the 'root' of anything, there is no sense of objective knowledge, it is all about intersubjectivity. It is very important that I recognize that because otherwise I get all caught up in trying to imagine I can reach some kind of objective knowledge that everyone can share in a complete sense, and that would be rather like seeking the holy grail. If I recognize what is happening in this hermeneutic circle of coming to an understanding, then I recognize that the knowledge that is being generated between people, negotiating meanings in an intersubjective way, is the closest I will get to objective knowledge.

I believe that it is a multiple socially constructed reality; in other words, everyone has their own view on what they perceive reality to be. But if we have different constructions as individuals, how can we 'get to know' other people's constructions? With such a view, there has to be a particular relationship going on between the researcher and the people that are being researched. The respondents are approached by the researcher as equal partners, with respect, because the interpretive researcher's task is to make sense of their world, to understand it, to see what meaning is imbued in that situation by the people who are part of it. I research the meanings and experiences of the people who function in the cultural web I study. As Geertz (1993: 5) puts it,

> Believing, with Max Weber, that man is an animal suspended in webs of significance he himself has spun, I take culture to be those webs, and the analysis of it to be therefore not an experimental science in search of a law but an interpretive one in search of meaning.

From the interaction between myself as the investigator and others as the investigated through which understanding is reached, meanings are constructed and interpreted. Talk has become the primary medium through which social interaction takes place. Our social world has become a conversational world and, since the insights of Wittgenstein and others, we resist the assumption that words are simply a transparent medium to reality. Wittgenstein tells us there is no direct route to others' 'inner experiences'. So although it is not possible to get inside someone else's head, or ever to really know how someone else feels, through empathetic understanding, gained by the sharing of a common language, we can dialogue, converse and share experiences.

All the things I have about me generate the knowledge that becomes my way of operating in the world. It is how I as a person apply this knowledge that impacts on how I behave and what I do. We generally do things as a result of how we see things and intend things or are motivated by things, and because we are knowledgeable we can discuss these things, talk about them, talk through them. Recognizing that helps me as a researcher to develop my methodology as an interpretive researcher.

Believing that I am capable of interpreting and articulating my experiences about the world to myself and others means I believe others can 'explain' themselves to me. I am therefore able to reconstruct the experiences of others in a way they recognize. I build a picture of the different voices, dialectically constructing a synthesis of the experience under study. The following extract from Ely (1991: 122) points out this relationship very well.

> The investigator wants to understand the minds and hearts of the research participants in as total and unadulterated a way as possible. To do so s/he must attempt to recognize personal prejudices, stereotypes, myths, assumptions, and other thoughts and feelings that may cloud or distort the perception of other people's experiences. I do not believe that we lose subjectivity, for human perception is by nature and definition subjective. I do believe that by recognising and acknowledging our own myths and prejudices, we can more effectively put them in their place. I also believe that greater self-knowledge can help us to separate out thoughts and feelings from those of our research participants, to be less judgmental, and to appreciate experiences that deviate greatly from our own.

The inquirer and the inquired into are interlocked in such a way that the findings of an investigation are the creation of the inquiring process. As Giddens (1993: 169) expresses it,

> The sociological observer cannot make social life available as a 'phenomenon' for observation independently of drawing upon her or his knowledge of it as a resource whereby it is constituted as a 'topic of investigation'. In this respect, the observer's position is no different from that of any other member of society; mutual knowledge is not a series of corrigible items, but represents the interpretative schemes which both sociologists and lay actors use, and must use, to 'make sense' of social activity – that is, to generate 'recognizable characterisations of it'.

Methodological implications

The way in which the theoretical approach and epistemological assumptions described in this chapter impact on my work as an educational researcher is reflected in the kinds of questions asked that initiate research practice. My perception of the educational activities I see around me are filtered by my theoretical and epistemological lenses. Interpreting the world as a researcher is a particular way of acting and doing in the very same social world in which we construct our lives. Given this recognition and also the ability to be reflexive and hence aware of our life view, then as researchers we can deal with what influences our research approach in a positive way. The researcher's orientation is an outcome of what interests and motivates and it provides the impetus for the style and thrust of the investigation. By way of illustration, two examples are offered here of research studies that indicate the theoretical and epistemological views expressed in this chapter. Both projects indicate my interest in grappling with the relationship between the valuing, meaning-attributing human and the educational structures they create and inhabit. Both studies are centrally concerned with coming to an understanding of the meanings imbued in the situation by the people who are part of it.

The first example is the project *Assessing Achievement in the Arts*. This project was funded by the Leverhulme Trust and came into being at the time of reform in the school curriculum with the introduction of the National Curriculum and a national standardized assessment system. Raising standards was the target and part of this was an objectively measured assessment system, a series of tests that, it was proclaimed by government, would act as a benchmark for the public to know whether standards were rising or falling. My colleague Malcolm Ross and I asked the question of how the arts would fare in these turbulent times and how the objectively based measurement-driven model of national assessment would 'fit' within the arts curriculum. In an educational world where the emphasis on assessing and reporting for accountability purposes predominated, we shared with many arts teachers a sense of unease over the assessment of creative work in schools. The central research questions in the project were organized around the creative challenge of devising a valid and comprehensive assessment strategy that would yield qualitative information about and do full justice to the pupils' artistic achievements. In the book that was one outcome of the project we expressed our research orientation as follows:

> The project on which this book is based aimed to give the pupils a voice, a place, in the assessment of their aesthetic activities and, at the same time, to allow the teacher's assessment to take full account of the pupils' subjective worlds – the world where their particular aesthetic projects are conceived and their unique aesthetic judgements made. Traditionally, 'subjectivity' (of the pupil and of the teacher-assessor) has been a problem for teaching and assessment in the arts. This is because arts teachers operate largely outside their pupils' expressive acts. We, for our part, have made subjectivity central in our account of assessment in the arts. Our chosen vehicle is pupil–teacher *talk*: assessment in and through conversation . . . we believe that talk not only provides a rich and highly appropriate means of learning more about our pupils' learning; it also serves to empower the pupils, to engage and involve themselves more directly in the assessment process. We shall go further and

> propose that the emphasis in the evaluation of arts practice should pass (and indeed may confidently be passed) to the pupils themselves. At the very least we would expect a 'negotiated' outcome to what has to be a collaborative undertaking in which formative appraisals – the very stuff of the teaching–learning process – provide the living ground of summative assessments.
>
> (Ross *et al.* 1993: xi–xii)

The second example is the project *Local Education Authorities: Accountability and Control*, which was funded by Joseph Rowntree. This project came into being as a result of the profound changes arising from the 1988, 1992 and 1993 Education Acts with respect to the formal relationship between central and local government in the education sector. My colleague Stephen Ball and I wanted to investigate the new forms of accountability and control developing within local settings that were emerging because of the changes. Our orientation is clearly expressed in our research report.

> Through a series of case studies of LEAs we explore the interpretation and enactment of change and assess the implications of these changes for the effective planning of local schools systems and for local accountability and democracy in education. Four key questions were asked in the research.
>
> - How have the roles and structures of LEAs altered in response to the redistribution of powers and responsibilities since 1988, and what are the consequences of these alterations for the 'culture and philosophy' of Authorities?
> - What factors are associated with the differences between LEAs in the ways in which they 'inhabit' and enact their new roles and structures?
> - What methods of intervention, influence and planning do LEAs now employ in their relations with schools, parents, national government and government agencies?
> - What are the forms and methods of accountability now being established within local systems of education?
>
> These are complex and open ended questions which cannot be answered simply nor can they be separated from the general and thorough-going changes in local government. Therefore the body of the report focuses, at different levels and in different contexts, on the issue of democratic accountability. We suggest that in the current legislative framework the meaning and practice of accountability are increasingly diverse, elusive and unclear. Some of the meanings and practices are explored. The report concludes with some considerations which point to a regeneration of the debate about the future of local democratic accountability.
>
> (Radnor and Ball 1996: 6)

Concluding thoughts

> Only societies reflexively capable of modifying their institutions in the face of accelerated social change will be able to confront the future with any confidence. Sociology is the prime medium of such reflexivity.
>
> (Giddens 1990: 21)

People create change, not social scientists. The educationalist researching from an interpretivist perspective is acting within a reflexive frame of reference. The next part of this book offers a way of undertaking interpretive research. Through engaging in this approach, I believe the knowledge gained is a resource which can be drawn upon in the process of managing our professional lives and coping with educational change. This enables us to understand our position in society and gives us the framework to interpret our world and to act upon it.

Part 2 | Undertaking interpretive research

Part 2 covers the methodological principles of interpretive research that follow from the theoretical framework given in Part 1, practices that follow from these principles and issues that arise from the practices of undertaking research the interpretive way. There are three chapters. Chapter 3 is concerned with how you approach the practice. Three main principles of researcher practice are the subject of the first part of the chapter. These principles guide the researcher on how to behave, and lead on to a discussion about inductive research design, which includes reference to the minimization of threats to the trustworthiness of the data collecting process and the validity of interpretation. The chapter ends with two examples of practice to illuminate the approach. Chapter 4 is entitled 'Watch, listen, ask, record' and deals with the practice of observing and interviewing, with examples from the research students. Chapter 5, entitled 'Analysis and interpretation', is dedicated to a practical model of analysis of qualitative data using interview data as exemplar material, and discusses the way in which interpretation follows on from descriptive analysis. Each chapter contains questions and activities to help you assimilate the process of undertaking interpretive research.

3 | Approaching practice

Part 1 has strongly indicated the central tenet of interpretive research, which is trying to come to an understanding of the world of the research participants and what that world means to them. This necessitates going into their setting and experiencing the environment in which they create their reality. David Morley (1992: 193) reminds us of the significance of knowing people in their socio-cultural environment with this metaphor:

> To draw a carp, Chinese masters warn, it is not enough to know the animal's morphology, study its anatomy or understand the physiological functions of its existence. They tell us that it is also necessary to consider the reed against which the carp brushes each morning while seeking its nourishment, the oblong stone behind which it conceals itself, or the rippling of water when it springs toward the surface. These elements should in no way be treated as the fish's environment, the milieu in which it evolves or the natural background against which it can be drawn. They belong to the carp itself.

Qualitative information is the essence of interpretive research, and observing the research participants in their social world and talking to them are the ways in which the majority of the data which shape the research interpretation are collected. Put simply, the researcher goes and talks to people about aspects of their lives. But, given the ontological and epistemological premises articulated in Part 1 of this book, what principles of researcher behaviour guide the practice of the interpretive researcher as he or she goes to find out about the thoughts and feelings of others? As human subjects researching other human subjects we have the capacity to be the best and the worst of researchers. The principles of researcher practice which act as a code of conduct should encourage good practice and, further, these principles should also inform the structure of the research design generated to carry out the research endeavour itself.

This chapter first describes these principles, then it discusses the way the research is designed to produce a research study that is in harmony with these principles. Second, in order to demonstrate how these principles interrelate with the structure of the design, the two research studies mentioned in Chapter 2 are revisited. These provide examples of the way educational research is approached when conducted in the interpretive way.

Principles of researcher practice

The principles can be summarized in the following statement.

> ***The researcher is the research instrument who engages in a transactional process, recognizing that the process is ethics-in-action.***

Principle 1 Researcher as data collecting instrument: the reflexive subject

Saying the researcher is the research instrument has significant implications for the researcher's roles and responsibilities. How does the researcher approach the research process and behave towards the research participants?

Educational research is generally undertaken by people who have a history of involvement in the field of education in a capacity other than that of researcher. In the main researchers in education are education managers or administrators, teachers or lecturers, and participate in research as a means to enhance their career and/or improve their understanding of issues that, it is hoped, help them to be better professionals. The researcher, therefore, is bringing to the research and is influenced by informal, personal and tacit theory about education. This has to be recognized and when recognized enhances the whole process of engaging in interpretive research. It becomes a positive aspect in research where the researcher is the research instrument ultimately in control of the research design she constructs. Maxwell (1996: 28) makes this point when he states that 'separating your research from other aspects of your life cuts you off from a major source of insights, hypotheses and validity checks.' Further, he quotes Peshkin, who has a realistic and positive way of making use of his personal, experiential knowledge:

> The subjectivity that originally I had taken as an affliction, something to bear because it could not be foregone, could, to the contrary, be taken as 'virtuous'. My subjectivity is the basis for the story that I am able to tell. It is a strength on which I build. It makes me who I am as a person and as a researcher, equipping me, from the selection of topics clear through to the emphases I make in my writing. Seen as virtuous, subjectivity is something to be capitalised on, rather than to exorcise.
>
> (Glesne and Peshkin 1992: 104)

This taking responsibility for the work from inception to fruition is the hallmark of the interpretive researcher. In the process of watching, listening, asking and recording in the world of her research participants, the researcher hones her skills as data collector, observing, taking notes, interviewing and all the time bringing her knowledge and intellect to the proceedings. In discussing the researcher as the major instrument Eisner (1988: 197) makes three important points:

> In the first place, many things that might be significant might not find a place on a formal observation schedule. One might not know in advance what is significant. Second, the meaning of an incident within a social situation might only be revealed by putting it in its historical context. No instrument which I know of can do this. Third, the expressive character of action and speech – their muted messages – are often so subtle that only a perceptive eye and an informed mind are likely to recognize their significance. Balance, tradeoff, context, and other features of social life must be considered if the interpretation of socially shared meanings is to have validity.

The researcher sorts and analyses the data, recognizing that although there are tools to assist her in the process, it is the researcher that is constantly, at each stage, making sense of things and decisions about the next steps. The researcher cannot remove her own way of seeing from the process, but she can engage reflexively in the process and be aware of her interpretive framework. Greta, discussing her methodology in her PhD study of Romanian teachers training to be teachers of English, deals with this issue very clearly and succinctly:

> Reflexivity is related to subjectivity and the researcher's effects on the process and on participants. It was difficult to disentangle these influences, but I have worked towards becoming aware of them and understanding them. I take into consideration the advantages and disadvantages of being immersed in the field which calls for a detailed examination of my personal experience with the field, the school culture and teaching. A clearer understanding of my own views on teaching and professional learning have led in the end to a critical distance from the data and my own deeply embedded cultural assumption helped by selecting participants with contrasting school backgrounds and experiences, implicit theories and learning styles. I have passed through a process of becoming aware of and of analysing mistakes, misunderstandings, doubts and other personal mishaps or flaws in collecting and analysing data. Also I have explored my position as a researcher with reference to the area and topic of research and with regard to the way I interacted with the material. The reflexive process implies listening to and understanding what the respondents were

> telling me. Categories are not imposed on them. I have had to find a mode of writing that would reflect the variety, diversity, as well as the uniqueness of the cases presented, dealing with and presenting 'the subtleties of meanings that emerged' (Radnor 1994: 10).

She concludes this section by quoting Steier (1991: 7).

> by holding our own assumed research structures and logics as themselves researchable and not immutable, and by examining how we are a part of our data, our research becomes, not a self-centred product, but a reciprocal process. The voices of those with whom we interact, our reciprocators (a calling I prefer), respondents, informants and subjects, are enhanced rather than lessened. Rather than being narcissistic, we become, through taking reflexivity seriously, social constructionist researchers. (Draft of methodology chapter to supervisor.)

Principle 2 Interpretive research as transactional: keep focus and interface data and developing ideas

It is the researcher's responsibility to engage in transactions with the participants in their own natural setting. With respect to educational research is it more often than not the case that both the research participants and the researcher share a common culture: that is, they understand each other, in the sense that they are all part of the education system. Given this common culture, the issue of gaining entry into the particular environment of the research participants and initiating a rapport should be less problematic than it would be going into an alien environment. The climate of interaction and the researcher's attitude and approach to the people in her study should convey to these people the confidence that they are going to be listened to without prejudice. The establishment of a trustworthy basis is important on at least two counts. One, it should encourage the research participants to say what they really feel, particularly if they are enabled by the researcher to be as clear as possible about what they are talking about. Two, the researcher should be able to revisit the research participants to develop the research, feeding back findings for discussion, clarification and so on.

The word transactional is used here to denote the nature of the interactions that go on in interpretive research in educational settings. The nature of the interactions operate on two levels. The first level is the practical one of researcher–research participants. The second level is the cognitive one of researcher–conceptual context. Maxwell (1996: 4) describes the conceptual context as:

> What do you think is going on with the phenomena you plan to study? What theories, findings and conceptual frameworks relating to these

phenomena will guide or inform your study, and what literature, preliminary research and personal experience will you draw on?

Therefore, at this second level, the researcher is all the time reflecting on what she is doing in association with what she knows and thinks about the phenomena under study.

On the practical level, saying the researcher transacts with the research participants, I wish to make a point about the nature of these transactions in terms of how much the researcher is in control of what she is doing. I shall do this by using the analogy of a business meeting in which the researcher is equivalent to the chairperson of the meeting and the participants are members of the meeting. The chair has set the agenda but once the meeting gets under way there is no guarantee that she will be able to go through that agenda item by item and receive the kind of responses that fit into her scheme of things. Power and control, in practice, are shared. The chair holds a form of power in that she controls the agenda and also writes the minutes! However, the members of the meeting have not necessarily sanctioned the agenda and might not share the chair's priorities. There is power in their ability to seize the initiative, rework the agenda and engage in a discourse on their own terms. The sensitivity of the researcher as the equivalent of the chairperson in the meeting is to be able to act in a democratic way and to negotiate, grasping as much of her participants' reality as possible, rather than trying to force her version of their reality on to them. So although she needs to be aware of the focus of her study and able to articulate what it is she wants to find out, she also needs to be flexible and open enough to rethink her strategies to meet the needs of the participants as research subjects. That is the meaning of engaging in a transactional process on a practical level.

On the cognitive level, as well as her personal knowledge she has made herself knowledgeable about existing theories in the public domain pertinent to her topic of investigation. The theories that exist about the topic are made up of a set of concepts interrelated in some way that tells you something about the topic. The identification of these concepts and of the theories themselves provides the theoretical framework that drives the thinking of the researcher, helping her to make sense of the data coming at her in the field. In the transactional process she is constantly interrelating what she is seeing/hearing in the field with the concepts relevant to the topic under investigation.

For example, in my own PhD study, which was an investigation into the way teachers implemented a new national examination in the structure of schooling, I read theories about the implementation of change in school settings. What I was seeing in the field as an interpretive researcher resonated with the findings of Ball (1987) in his study of the organizational life of a school. His model of theorizing, a micro-political perspective, gave me a purchase on my data that related epistemologically to an interactionist/interpretive approach to research. Ball wrote that 'Micro-politics recognises constraints, but it also focuses upon what people do by way of shaping the social relations they live by' (Ball 1987: 279). Micro-politics rests on the conception of organizations 'driven' by individual and collective interests. The micro-political perspective, through focusing on individuals and groups of social actors, illuminates interpersonal processes by drawing on such concepts as control, goal diversity, ideology and conflict. Having a theory to frame my analysis and also identifying key concepts that would help to sensitize me to what was happening in the field, I was able to conceptualize what I was seeing/hearing. I was highly conscious that I was not collecting information in a theoretical vacuum. These concepts gave me a framework in which I could start to formulate ideas about what was happening, which is quite different from saying I had a hypothesis to refute or verify.

A way of dealing with these developing ideas that emanate from this transactional research process is to write analytic memos. Maxwell (1996: 12) puts it very well:

> Memos are one of the most important techniques you have for developing your own ideas. You should therefore think of memos as a way to help you understand your topic, setting, or study, not just as a way of recording or presenting an understanding you've already reached. Memos should include reflections on your reading and ideas, as well as your fieldwork. Write memos as a way of working on a problem you have in making sense of your topic, setting, or study. Write memos whenever you have an idea that you want to develop further, or simply to record the idea for later development. Write lots of memos, throughout the course of your research project.

Principle 3 Interpretive research is ethics-in-action: dignity and respect for participants

The researcher as instrument transacting in the field is qualitatively dependent on the relationships initiated and developed by the researcher with the research participants. The principle of ethics-in-action focuses centrally on the need for the researcher to show respect for the participants. The participants are subjects, not samples or representatives of a larger population. The ethical guidelines of the British Educational Research Association (BERA) have five clauses, clauses 7–11, devoted to ethical approaches to research participants.

> *Responsibility to the participants*
>
> 7 Participants in a research study have the right to be informed about the aims, purposes and likely publication of findings involved in the research and of potential consequences for participants, and to give their informed consent before participating in research.

8 Care should be taken when interviewing children and students up to school leaving age; permission should be obtained from the school, and if they so suggest, the parents.
9 Honesty and openness should characterise the relationship between researchers, participants and institutional representatives.
10 Participants have the right to withdraw from a study at any time.
11 Researchers have a responsibility to be mindful of cultural, religious, gendered, and other significant differences within the research population in the planning, conducting, and reporting of their research.

The manifestation of the ethical approach in research practice is for the researcher to take the attitude that as she is entering their setting, it is necessary to reach mutual agreement about what constitutes good conduct in the situation. Greta in her interpretive PhD study, exploring learner teachers' thinking and the process of learning to teach, summarizes her consideration of ethical issues to, as she put it, 'protect her respondents':

- confidentiality and anonymity were respected – respondents received different names from the real ones and any information in the interviews or diaries was deleted if it was so personal as to lead to respondent identification, but was not relevant for the study;
- interpersonal interaction occurred in a natural, unobtrusive and non-threatening manner;
- observing and interviewing the participants in their own settings;
- collaboration in building mutual trust and understanding;
- description of potential benefits on both sides;
- right to withdraw from the study at any time and to decide on the degree of self-disclosure, without any personal prejudice or consequences (personal correspondence with supervisor October 2000).

Greta's approach to her participants in her study matches the tenor of the BERA guidelines and also indicates the sensitivity of her approach, concomitant with the two other principles of researcher practice described above. In a discussion of ethics in undertaking research, the approach of Pring (1984: 10) clearly expresses the principle of ethics-in-action, respecting the participants through setting up the process of feeding back data and sharing findings with them:

> At the outset of a research project, the investigation should set out clearly the kinds of knowledge sought and re-negotiate these as the project evolves. Second, the researcher is obliged to declare throughout the project, the data being collected and the interpretations put on them. Third, the researcher should be continuously open to cross-examination by subjects on points of objectives, methodology, interpretations and so on. Fourth, those researched are entitled to have their response included with the published report.

Research design

So what would a research design look like to comply with these principles? Design can be described in a number of different ways but here I use the description preferred by Maxwell (1996: 1–2), which emphasizes the way the different components need to balance one with another: 'An underlying scheme that governs functioning, developing and unfolding and the arrangement of elements or details in a product or a work of art' (*Merrian Webster's Collegiate Dictionary*). An interpretive design is the scheme that provides the structure whereby the researcher shapes ideas, and it should reflect the structure of the hermeneutic circle, the process of interpretation, reflection and reinterpretation leading to an understanding. If the hermeneutic circle was represented as a three-dimensional object it would resemble a coiled ceramic pot. In the art and craft of pottery there is a technique called coiling, in which sausage-shaped ropes of clay are built one on the other and blended together to make a rounded object, the size of object dependent on the size of the base and the number and size of the coils. The making of a pot through the technique of coiling is a useful analogy for interpretive research design.

The clay that is used by the potter is not that which is found in its natural state, but has other materials added to it so that it can behave in the way required to make pots. This produced clay, the raw material for hand sculpting, is analogous to the conceptual context–data interaction, the raw material of the research process.

Ball (1993: 45), in discussing data, states: 'Data are a social construct of the research process itself, not just of the "natives" under study. Data are a product of the skills and imagination of the researcher and of the interface between the researcher and the researched.' As the clay is the raw material with which the potter's hand sculpts, the conceptual context/data is the raw material with which the researcher's mind sculpts.

The potter makes the coil	The researcher collects the data
The potter attaches the coil to the base then adds coil to coil	The researcher analyses the data then collects more data and analyses again
The potter blends a new coil to an existing coil	The researcher interprets from the analysis so far
The potter repeats the process until the form is complete and an object results	The researcher repeats the process of collecting, analysing and interpreting until a picture emerges worthy of presentation

The analogy is a useful one because, first, it highlights rigour and artistry and, second, it focuses our minds on key characteristics of interpretive design, namely:

- a balance between data collecting and analysis/interpretation;
- emphasis on the here and now, on lived experience;
- working with the 'raw material' in an interactive and sensitive way – data and conceptual context;
- the unfolding of a holistic picture.

As with the pot, the developing structure will determine the ultimate shape because, during the ongoing process, the researcher moulds and shapes the data in a dialectical relationship with the conceptual context to generate some substantive theory that holds together. In other words, as Geertz (1993: 27) describes it,

> the meaning that the particular actions have for the actors whose actions they are and stating as explicitly as we can manage what the knowledge thus attained demonstrates about the society in which it is found and beyond that, about social life itself.

During the process of making the pot, the potter is always judging whether or not the pot is holding together, asking, 'Does it look aesthetically pleasing? Is it going to work as a pot?' and so on. This process of evaluation is also true of the researcher, asking, 'Why should people take my ideas seriously? Is this research study any good?' This issue of whether the study is a good one takes us into criteria of quality. We need to ask the question: 'How should the interpretive study be judged?' In asking this question we need to remember that we recognize that social life is an interpreted world, not a literal one. A particular view of what constitutes knowledge within this perspective is accepted as the basic premise from which to generate criteria. Hammersley (1992) provides the notion of 'subtle realism', which is useful to encapsulate the underlying approach to knowledge that guides the criteria for quality.

> This subtle realism retains from naïve realism the idea that research investigates independent knowable phenomena. But it breaks with it in denying that we have direct access to those phenomena, in accepting that we must always rely on cultural assumptions, and in denying that our aim is to reproduce social phenomena in some way that is uniquely appropriate to them. Obversely, subtle realism shares with scepticism and relativism a recognition that all knowledge is based on assumptions and purposes and is a human construction, but it rejects these positions' abandonment of the regulative idea of independent and knowable phenomena. Perhaps most important of all, subtle realism is distinct

> from both naïve realism and relativism in its rejection of the notion that knowledge must be defined as beliefs whose validity is known with certainty.
>
> (Hammersley 1992: 52)

Geertz (1993: 28–9) offers the story of an Englishman in India who was told that the world rests on a platform which rests on the back of an elephant which rests on the back of a turtle. He asked, what did the turtle rest on? Another turtle. And that turtle? Ah Sahib, after that it is turtles all the way down. The point here is that it is impossible to get to 'the bottom of things', but you can try to get as far down the turtle chain as you can. Given this position, we can frame our question. *What should the criteria be to assess the quality of interpretive research?* In reflecting on my own work I summarize my criteria as, first, trust in the data collection process and, second, validity in the interpretation.

Trust in data collection and analysis

The key criterion is trust.

> Focusing on trustworthiness rather than truth displaces validation from its traditional location in a presumably objective, non-reactive and neutral reality and moves it to the social world – a world constructed in and through our discourse and actions, through praxis.
>
> (Mishler 1990: 420)

Under this criterion, the response to the question 'What makes a good interpretive qualitative research study?' is that it has explanatory and illuminating power about the situation under study, uncovering a multiplicity of individual perceptions about the situation and increasing understanding of issues that are present in the situation. For the explanations to be considered 'robust' they should be justified by making reference to the data which should be of good quality if collected following the principles of the procedures outlined above.

The first principle of procedure includes the following statement. 'The researcher cannot remove her own way of seeing from the process but she can engage reflexively in the process and be aware of her interpretive framework.' This is fundamentally about researcher integrity. She accounts for herself as researcher and in the process of the writing of the research enters into a dialogue with the reader. The I of the researcher is apparent and the nature of the research process offered. The reader should be able to catch sight of how the research was done. It is important to include the researcher's entry into the context, i.e. her role, the kind of data collected and the way they were analysed. The researcher must build confidence in her integrity as a researcher trying to represent faithfully and accurately the social worlds or phenomena studied.

The second principle of procedure includes the following statement. 'The climate of interaction, the researcher's attitude and approach to the people in her study should convey to these people the confidence that they are going to be listened to without prejudice. The establishment of a trustworthy basis.' An understanding by the reader of how this rapport was established and trust generated raises the confidence of the reader in the credibility of the findings.

The third principle includes the following statement: 'The principle of ethics-in-action focuses centrally on the need for the researcher to show respect for the participants.' This is mainly achieved through member checks that make sure that the research respondents' constructed realities are represented. This helps to confirm the data as trustworthy evidence on which interpretations are made.

In discussing issues of the trustworthiness of her research, Greta describes a number of steps she took to minimize threats to trustworthiness which she believes helps to give a robustness to her analysis and interpretation and hence increases a belief in the validity of her interpretation. She outlines them as follows:

1 Participants were explained the broad objectives of the research and were assured of confidentiality. Time was devoted to developing the trust and confidence of the student teachers to ensure the authenticity of information and honest cooperation.
2 Data were gathered using various techniques, which ensured data-source and technique triangulation (Hammersley and Atkinson 1983).
3 In order to enable readers to assess the trustworthiness of the research I have provided an honest and explicit description of the research process and the methods used in collecting and analysing the data.
4 The interactive and iterative nature of data collection and analysis enabled constant elaboration and verification of interpretations. Tentative interpretations could be tested against further data that were collected and some open-ended questioning in follow-up interviews was used to clarify or verify previous information.
5 When case histories were assembled, key informants were asked to read transcripts and their own case interpretation for 'respondent verification'. They had to pay attention to the accuracy of the interpretations and to make comments.
6 Awareness of my own familiarity with the context led to the need for distancing myself from the context and data. Continued readings of the source materials at different times led to verification of presuppositions and interpretations (Personal correspondence with supervisor, November 2000).

Validity of interpretation

As researchers, we account for ourselves in the way we write up our studies. Meanings and definitions are brought to actual situations and are produced through a communication process. A sense of honesty is displayed in the way that the researcher holds on to the value of integrity and communicates to the reader that she has tried to provide an account that is as close to the subjects' rendering of the situation as she is capable of understanding it. Validity of the findings is helped by being able to separate a descriptive analysis from interpretation. The descriptive analysis enables the reader to gain a picture of the subjects under study – hear their words, get a sense of their actions and their context and know that there is more where that came from. Consciousness that there is evidence to support the interpretation generates confidence in the bases of the researcher's interpretation. The interpretive process is an act of conceptualization that informs the acts of the individuals. The unique situation is illuminated and at the same time insights are conveyed that exceed the limits of the situation from which they emerge. Maxwell (1992) distinguishes between internal generalizability, which refers to the generalizability of a conclusion within the setting of a group studied, and external generalizability, which goes beyond the setting. For example, in my own PhD study (1996), where as part of the research I was studying the interactions between curriculum team leaders and their team, my account would have lacked interpretive validity if I had only observed interactions between selective members of the team rather than all members. External generalizability within qualitative research refers to the ability of the study to develop theory that can be extended to other cases. So although my case study research could not say anything about the representativeness of its sample, it derives its validity from the thoroughness of its analysis. This thorough analysis can lead to theoretical propositions. In the case of my PhD the analysis came up with a theoretical proposition around the notion of accommodation, which linked an externally imposed assessment development with the management of change literature. This has made an empirical contribution to the understanding of how school reform is accommodated by the key actors-teachers, providing a perspective that causes pause for thought to those policy-makers who argue that measurement really can drive instruction. Thus it is possible, having generated this conceptualization, abstracted from the particular case, to apply it and see if it has purchase beyond this study. Bryman (1988: 91), using Glaser and Strauss's discussion of 'awareness context' in relation to dying in hospital, makes this same point:

> The issue of whether the particular hospital studied is 'typical' is not the critical issue; what is important is whether the experiences of dying patients are typical of the broad class of phenomena . . . to which the

theory refers. Subsequent research would then focus on the validity of the proposition in other milieux.

As demonstrated in the above discussion about research design, there is an interplay between the design components and the principles of researcher practice, which operates in a cyclical process leading to an explanation of the phenomena under study. In the following discussion of two research projects, the way that the design and principles interrelate in practice can be further illuminated.

Example 1 Assessing achievement in the arts

The way the researchers conducted themselves in this project and the design process of the research itself are practical examples of the theoretical explanations offered in the first part of this chapter, particularly with respect to recognizing the teacher as a purposive agent capable of generating change. The research methods in the project were qualitative, with the emphasis on participant observation of classroom practice and interviewing of teachers and pupils. The data were collected by means of audio and video recordings as well as written notes. At various stages during the project the findings were fed back to the participants through one-day conferences at strategic times between the different project phases. This allowed for responses from conference participants to be incorporated into the next phase of the project. The project had four phases, with each phase developing out of the analysis of the data gathered in the preceding phase. This enabled the researchers to respond to the findings of each stage and to adjust the direction of the project to address predominant issues that emerged through the empirical evidence. After the final phase, analytically descriptive case studies based upon the written, oral and videotaped material were written up to illuminate the final interpretive commentary.

The approach of the research team, which consisted of four members, was to spend the initial period of the project sharing their individual personal, experiential knowledge about the topic. Alongside the process of generating the research design, discussions took place that uncovered the values, attitudes, biases and knowledge about the issue of assessment in the arts. Each member of the team saw herself or himself as a research instrument. The research assistants were not just an operative for each research director but had a full participatory role in the design and development of the project. The principle of research as transactional is clearly visible in this project. This is at the practical level of the relationship with the teachers but also at the cognitive level. The team were constantly engaging in discussions about the conceptual context. This was an ongoing process, developing differently as the research itself developed. Certain theories and conceptual frameworks guided and informed the study. The project was guided by a notion of the aesthetic that connected with coming to an understanding of children's subjective experiencing in the arts. The project team found it helpful to conceptualize the aesthetic as a mode of cognition, a way of knowing; not a condition of being, but a process, an operation, a way of engaging in the world, a form of work. The aesthetic became a description of a form of experiencing, so the focus became aesthetic knowing, aesthetic responding, aesthetic perceiving, aesthetic understanding. All of these are constructive and constitutive activities, ways of becoming as well as ways of being. Having an aesthetic response is about a way of looking at things. The way that language is used in describing and discussing an aesthetic response was also articulated because the nature of talk was so central to this study. The project was informed in its data analysis by ideas developed by Rom Harré (1983). His conceptual framework, which links personal development to the expressive dimension of human behaviour, gave the project a purchase on the conversations between teachers and pupils.

This project was carried out in close collaboration with teachers. Teachers were not simply respondents to a research process controlled by the research team, but many became collaborators, with their interactions and ideas helping to form and shape the design exposition. They were fully informed about each aspect of the research, free to withdraw at any time and treated with honesty and openness across each phase. Mutual trust and understanding was crucial as, during the later phases of the study, research could not be undertaken without very purposive engagement by both teachers and pupils. By the end of the project, 82 conversations had been videotaped. This would not have been possible without negotiation between the various parties and sensitive behaviour on the part of the researchers. The design components described below give a flavour of the research process.

The study spanned four phases, each consisting of data collection, analysis and interpretation.

Phase 1 (time span four months)

This involved identification of teachers agreeing to be part of the project: 25 teachers across eight schools in the south-west of England participated: five art, seven music, eight drama, one dance and four English teachers. They were visited, interviewed and observed teaching. The initial research question they were asked was, 'What do you consider to be the central concerns of your own particular arts subject?' The majority of the teachers referred especially to the expressive and creative opportunities offered to the pupils in the arts. When they were asked how pupils dealt with these opportunities, the teachers stated that they found the expressive/creative areas elusive, difficult to define and inadequately addressed by existing assessment procedures, which concentrated upon easily quantifiable and observable processes and products. The project classroom observation identified the ways the teachers provided an environment for their pupils to engage in artistic endeavours, how they talked to them and how they assessed their work. As well as being observed in their classrooms, the teachers were interviewed in order that the researchers could come to an understanding of each teacher's ideological perspective on assessment and the reasons why they operated assessment as they did. The phase ended when the project began to shape up around the idea of redressing the balance between the observable/quantifiable and the tacit/unquantifiable in assessment in order to seek ways in which the personal experience of pupils could properly be identified and valued. The researchers worked alongside the teachers in developing an assessment strategy that more closely resembled, reflected and could be integrated with the facilitative role they adopted when teaching.

Phase 2 (time span four months)

This phase began with a one-day evaluative conference between the project team and the project teachers. The conference decided that the project should explore 'talk' as a medium of assessment. The notion of an assessment conversation between pupils and teacher emerged. The teachers were asked to engage in a conversation with their pupils that focused on their arts work. The guidance was articulated as follows:

> The purpose of the conversation is to discuss with the student their understanding of the process which is ongoing. This is to encourage the pupil to self-assess in a formative way that will give her/him the confidence to continue to develop her/his arts work. The conversation should, therefore, be task-oriented, i.e. specific to a particular piece of work.

The conversations were recorded on video and audio tape so that they could (a) be discussed with the participants and (b) be analysed by the researchers.

Phase 3 (time span four months)

As a consequence of phase 2 the researchers developed a sense of both the nature of the assessment conversation and its content. At this stage the word 'aesthetic' was adopted to describe the principle focus of interest. The project workers wrote a booklet for the project's teachers, setting out their account of aesthetic understanding and suggesting key aspects of a conversation that could assess pupil's aesthetic understanding. Teachers were now being asked to engage in a process possibly different from their usual behaviour. There needed to be trust and respect between the researchers and the teachers to enable them to take risks, as well as trust and respect between teachers and pupils for the pupils to feel able to talk openly about how they feel, and to believe that their evaluative comments and judgements were taken seriously. The teachers engaged in assessment conversations with pupils and the encounters were videotaped and discussed by researchers and teachers.

Phase 4 (time span three months)

Findings of phase 3 were discussed with the teachers and it was agreed to try to communicate some of the ideas that emerged from the project to a new set of teachers. Arts teachers from four schools were approached and material was sent to them in advance of a full day's session to introduce them to the project. Following this, assessment conversations were recorded between teacher and pupil. The project team had interpreted a need for developing an assessment construct that gave a place to aesthetic understanding and had attempted to meet that need. The research write-up illuminated an assessment strategy that presents an alternative vision of the purpose and process of assessment that was itself evaluated by both the research team and their teacher collaborators. A worthy outcome for a piece of interpretive research.

Example 2 Local education authorities: accountability and control

The way the researchers conducted themselves in this project and the design process of the research itself are practical examples of the theoretical explanations offered in the first part of this chapter. This is particularly with respect to the interplay between agency and structures. By means of researching the interpretive way it is possible to get beneath the surface of the formal structure to look at the constraints, tensions, incoherences and confusions that emanated from investigating the locus of control and accountability in the changing duties and responsibilities of local education authorities (LEAs). The research was undertaken because the researchers believed that the future roles and structures and organizational culture of LEAs remained unclear, and the relationships between local democracy and educational accountability were blurred and uncertain. They believed it was a mistake to assume that the impacts and effects of changes would be uniform across LEAs or that they would result in the total eradication of local government influence over educational planning. The previous and ongoing work of the researchers indicated that the history, politics and ethos of LEAs, the idiosyncrasies of local market dynamics and the history of social relations between LEAs and their schools would combine to produce significant differences in the mode of adaptation to change from one LEA to another, and differences in the extent of influence that any LEA was able to retain over the form and structure of its school system. In other words, the researchers wished to argue that LEAs 'inhabit' and enact change in different ways, and these differences have implications for the nature of accountability and democracy at local level.

The research methods in the project were qualitative, with the emphasis on researcher as observer and interviewer. The observation took place in LEA committee meetings, council meetings, school governor meetings, local and national meetings involving LEA officers, headteachers or governors that were deemed appropriate for the research and interviews of councillors, LEA officers, headteachers and governors. The data were collected by means of extensive note taking at meetings, alongside the collection of papers, minutes of meetings and documents. The interviews were semi-structured or open-ended, generally audiotaped and then transcribed. There were two phases to this research project, which was undertaken by a team of four researchers. Two researchers each concentrated on one LEA, one researcher concentrated on two LEAs and the fourth researcher undertook interviews in support of the other three. The team sent copies of the transcribed interviews to one another and met at regular interviews to share analysis and interpretation. The writing of the report was shared by the co-directors of the project.

Design components

During the first phase the focus of attention was at LEA level. As well as a general concern with recent changes in the structure and methods of local educational government and local educational relationships, the interviews explored three substantive policy and management issues: special educational provision, school inspection and the management of school places. These issues provided a means of gaining purchase on the changing patterns of accountability, relationships and responsibilities that were evolving in each of the authorities. At the end of this phase, at the point where the research focus shifted from the LEA's relationship with its schools to the schools' response to their LEA practices, a day conference for representatives of the LEA took place in order for the research team to feed back findings to date and to share interpretation of these findings with the LEA representatives. The findings discussed by the participants centred on a number of key issues about the nature of political control, the local history of the LEA, local structural idiosyncrasies, financial constraints and size. The responses from conference participants to the issues raised informed the writing-up of analytically descriptive case studies of each of the LEAs. The introduction of this section of the report reads:

> This section of the report concentrates on the processes of redefinition of the relationships that the four LEAs have had with 'their' schools as

they come to terms with the new legislative arrangements outlined earlier and attempt to come to terms with the various legal, political and educational responsibilities.

(Radnor and Ball 1996: 11)

The second phase of the research concentrated on the school level, looking at the issues from the perspective of the headteachers. Eighteen interviews took place with headteachers in infant, junior and secondary schools in each LEA. All these interviews were semi-structured and lasted between 40 and 60 minutes. The key questions asked of headteachers concerned their perceptions of the role of the LEA, the impact the changes had had on their relationship with their LEA, their view of LEA services and to whom they now felt accountable. Governor data were also collected through group discussion with governors, notes taken at governor meetings in the schools where the headteachers were interviewed, regional and national governor conferences and some individual semi-structured interviews. Governors were asked to describe their relationships with their headteacher and the LEA, their working practices with their head, their views on accountability and their understanding of their legal position. All the interviewees received copies of their transcribed interviews for comment. The section of the report discussing the findings from this phase cut across the four LEA case studies. The reason for this was that the distribution of responses from headteachers was unrelated to the nature, history and politics of LEA organization or arrangements, and more related to personal and institutional relationships between the school and the authority. Some general patterns emerged across the schools and LEAs, so it made more sense following the analysis to write this section under the headings of headteacher relationships with the LEA, headteacher responses to LEA provision and working relationships with their governing bodies.

Following this phase an invitation seminar took place, entitled 'Looking to the Future'. The seminar was designed to bring the findings of the research to the attention of representatives from LEAs, headteachers, governors and parent and teacher associations.

The thrust of the research was to focus at different levels on the issue of democratic accountability and to try to come to an analytical understanding of the evolving methods, problems and relationships of LEAs. The final section of the report takes up the issue of accountability at LEA level and suggests three models of accountability that emerged from the research. The models are termed emergent/transitional because of the recognition of continuing change and also because the issues of democratic accountability are confused and cross-cut by issues of service accountability. Nevertheless, the aim of the report, to offer an interpretive understanding of the meaning and practice of accountability, provided some illuminating insights into LEA–school relationships at a time of profound social change.

Concluding thoughts

This chapter has sought to show one researcher's perspective on interpretive research, with examples of practice to illustrate how the principles of researcher practice inform the design of the research. Four key questions are presented here to encourage the reader to think and reflect upon when considering his or her approach to working in the interpretive way.

Key questions

1. What stance do you take as a researcher towards your research context and the key research participants?
2. What are the key principles you need to grapple with in undertaking interpretive research?
3. What does the notion of interpreting data mean to you?
4. How do you judge that what you are doing is good?

4 | Watch, listen, ask, record

Watching what people do and say is a natural way for us to behave; we do it all the time in public and private settings. When we are interacting with people, we observe others in the situation in order to decide how we should respond to them. When we are in a public place observing people but not necessarily interacting with them we engage in 'people watching' because it reinforces our own behaviour, fascinates us, entertains us or even informs us how not to behave! Watching and listening can give us a sense of the social life of others. We can begin to recognize patterns of behaviour and the quality of relationships by observing the interactions between people. But if we want to understand what makes them do what they do then we need to ask them. Asking people takes us into the realm of meanings. In terms of interpretive research, the meanings that people attribute to the social situations in which they find themselves are important data. Consequently, a means whereby such information can be successfully collected is needed. The interview format serves this purpose because the interview is an interactive human encounter in which someone seeking information asks for it and, more often than not, is supplied with it by another. A combination of data collected through watching, listening, asking and recording – that is, observing and interviewing – enables us to engage in the act of interpretation. This chapter discusses first the strategies of observing and then those of interviewing that are most commonly used in the approach to interpretive research advocated in this book.

Watch, listen, record: observation

Morris (1973: 906) defines observation in a broad overarching way. Observation is 'the act of noting a phenomenon, often with instruments, and recording it for scientific and other purposes'. Watching and listening are part of our everyday life and are two basic ways in which we learn about our fellow beings. Utilizing these basic skills with a specific purpose and extra concentration, and recording what we see is observation for research purposes. Gold (1958) typifies four roles that the researcher can take in observing social settings. These are complete observer, observer as participant, participant as observer and complete participant. However, it has been argued that all social research is a form of participant observation because we cannot study social life without being part of it (Hammersley and Atkinson 1983). This is particularly the case in interpretive research where the researcher goes into the setting of the research participants. From this point of view participant observation is not a particular research technique but a mode of being-in-the world characteristic of researchers (Atkinson and Hammersley 1994). The decision the researcher takes, depending on the design of the study, is the level of participation that is deemed appropriate. The researcher needs to ask the questions, 'How do I observe these actors under study? What is the best way for me to do this in order to carry through in practice my research purposes?' Remembering that interpretive research is about coming to an understanding of the world of the research participants, the observation approach has to take the stance of seeing the social reality of the research setting as initially unknown and unknowable until the way the actors operate in their world is understood. As Polsky (1971: 126–7) writes:

> initially keep your eyes open and ears open and keep your mouth shut. At first try to ask no questions whatsoever. Before you ask questions, or even speak much at all other than when spoken to, you should get the 'feel' of their world by extensive and attentive listening – get some sense of their frame of reference, and some of their sense of language.

In this respect the observation techniques share many of the qualities of ethnographic practices. Ethnography is a detailed sociological observation of people which involves the researcher in an intense period of observation which guides and informs all subsequent data gathering. The approach discussed here, although taking the lead from ethnography in so far as following the same principles of good practice in observation techniques, is far less intense. Less time is available to spend in the field and other forms of data collecting, such as interviewing, usually take precedence.

It is often the case in the educational context that the observer is also an educator. This is important to take into consideration. The observer is in a familiar work location, observing people like herself, and in this situation is aware of her own experience of similar settings and how people behave in them. There is, as Douglas (1976) puts it, a 'general cultural understanding'. Having a cultural understanding means that the researcher can read the situation he or she is in with a greater degree of accuracy and in a shorter space of time than in a culturally unfamiliar setting. This can have either a positive or negative affect on the quality of the observation data. Looked at positively, the researcher can sensitively be responsive within the context, choosing the degree of participant observation to suit situations that arise. For example, in observing in a classroom, the researcher can make a professional judgement about whether it would be better for the researcher to be an observer as participant, i.e. to engage minimally in what is going on in the classroom, or to be a participant as observer, i.e. to get involved as the teacher's assistant. On the other hand, negatively, the background knowledge and experience of the researcher can have the affect of lulling the researcher into being a bit less conscientious in listening and making assumptions about what is going on, based on knowledge of educational contexts overall, rather than concentrating specifically on the one under study.

It is also worth recognizing that as an educator in an educational setting as observer there needs to be an awareness that probably he or she is perceived by the adults and the students in the setting as being an educator, whether it be another teacher or lecturer from a different institution or an adviser/manager coming to 'check them out', rather than simply a researcher intent on 'just finding out'. Others' ambiguous perceptions of the researcher need to be dealt with in as sensitive a way as possible in order to adhere to the principle of ethics-in-action.

Central to observing in the interpretive way is the notion of emergence. By that I mean that the researcher, in coming to an understanding of the situation, has to make sense of the context, has to be able to describe the context overall. The researcher works at recording what is happening in real time, as it happens. The aim is to try to understand the 'culture' of the social setting, the norms, values and habits that make up the way of behaving in this setting. There are no preset observational categories or structured observation schedules. That would contradict the notion of emergence, of finding out what emerges from the setting.

Activity

Undertake an observation of a group of people in a public place, a parents' meeting, an open evening, a shopping mall, a sports club etc. Watch them for about an hour. Make a note of the events that happen, the interactions of the members of the group, the tone of the interactions, body language, the ebb and flow of conversation, the relationships between members of the group and so on. Fix on a way to record your observations that gives a picture of the proceedings.

The detailed recording of the observations, i.e. writing them down, should be undertaken as soon as possible after leaving the field. It should not be left to the next day, as aspects will certainly be lost in the activities of daily life. The recording should be systematic, with headings and a record of time, place and the names of the people involved. If, for example, a meeting is being observed diagrams with the layout of the room are useful for descriptive purposes. The intention of this form of observation is to grasp what usually goes on in the setting so as to help you as researcher to be able to interpret social actions in their own context, and therefore to understand better the situation from the actors' point of view when they are interviewed. Observation integrated with interviewing produces an interpretive rendering of sounder quality. Adler and Adler (1994: 382) comment:

> Observation produces especially great rigor when combined with other methods. In contrast to experiments conducted in the laboratory that lack a natural setting and context of occurrence, and interviews with subjects that are constructions of subjects' recollection and (sometimes self-serving) perceptions, researchers' observations of their settings and subjects can be considered hard evidence. These are especially valuable as an alternative source of data for enhancing cross-checking (Douglas 1976) or triangulation (Denzin 1989) against information gathered through other means. Direct observation when added on to other research yielding depth/or breadth, enhances consistency and validity.

Descriptions of observer methods by the PhD students are presented below. The first two examples from Greta and Amany discuss how they came to the method they adopted, and explain how the data collected are used to support other approaches of data collecting, principally interviewing. The third example is a fuller account by Jean. This account indicates clearly the way that the principles of researcher practice become actual practice in carrying out observations the interpretive way. The writing-up of the observations by this student provides a description of how she conducted herself during the process and informs the reader about what she believes she as research instrument is taking into the setting. It exemplifies the notion of the transactional process and how she adheres to ethics-in-action.

Example 1 Greta's classroom observation of student teachers during their teaching practice

This narrative exemplifies:

- the value of open-ended observation;
- the use put to the data – supporting interviewing;
- sensitivity to the context;
- awareness of the culture.

Direct observation was used to explore what was going on in the classroom and to discover why the student teachers taught English the way they did. It was also used as a supportive technique to verify the data collected via diaries and interviews. The approach to observation that I finally adopted was not arrived at lightly. I had already piloted a systematic observation schedule with preset categories through observing one teacher and found that the schedule affected my ability to observe. The observation remained at surface level and missed the meaning that emerged from seeing the teacher's behaviour in its fullest context. I decided, instead, to take a more open-ended approach and to capture as many aspects of the teacher's work as possible. This approach allowed me considerable freedom in the kind of information I gathered. In opting for this kind of observation, I recognized that it required a conscious effort to distribute my attention widely and evenly, maintaining it at a high level.

The student teachers were observed during the period of their teaching practice, which consisted of four hours a week over a period of three months. They were required to observe classes, to teach up to four classes and to discuss them with their mentors. One or two of these classes were evaluated and assessed by the mentor for their final grade. For these reasons I was invited to and could observe only one or two classes with each participant. But irrespective of this constraint, the class observation offered opportunities to explore the student teachers' behaviour and classroom events in what would be a natural setting for them as teachers. It enabled, when not directly interacting with the student teachers, the opportunity of seeing them in action. These data were analysed for key episodes, which generated questions for the interviews. Backed up by interviews and diaries, it gave access to the respondents' interpretation of their actions, mental activities and perceptions.

Open-ended strategies were used for recording data, e.g. audio recording and field notes. The lessons were audiotaped and I also took notes for safety's sake, in case they were not well recorded. The participants were given the cassettes to listen to and to remind them of the lessons they had taught. Based on them I wrote narrative accounts of what had happened in the classroom. I was aware that personal observational biases might have distorted the information obtained and the interpretation of the classroom events. Being a member of the school culture, I had to be alert to the possibility that I could categorize classroom events on the basis of an assumed shared knowledge within the culture. I actively worked at minimizing possible observational biases by cross-checking the observation data with information in the interviews and diaries that referred to the same events. Field notes, repeated listening to the tapes and reading of diaries and interview transcripts helped me to bring to the fore the connotations the participants attached to events, and their interpretation was done within a framework of negotiated and shared meanings. Observing teachers at the initial stage of data collection also helped me to distance myself from my own teaching. I concentrated on understanding their teaching and their actions from their own perspectives.

Example 2 Amany's classroom observation of student teachers' professional studies lectures at their university in Egypt

This description exemplifies:

- observation to build an understanding of the context;
- observation to experience the teaching–learning environment;
- sensitivity towards the lecturers in the setting;
- the value of the open-ended observation approach made manageable by using time units;
- the use to which the observation data are put to support interviewing.

Observation was used because it is a main tool in helping the researcher to understand the context within which programme activities occur. It allows the observer to be inductive because she has less need to rely on prior conceptualizations of the setting. It provides opportunities for things that may routinely escape conscious awareness among participants in the programme to be revealed and then discussed. There is also the possibility that the observer can learn things that programme participants may be unwilling to talk about in an interview.

For the study of the professional education programmes of students training to be science teachers, observation was used to explore the physical setting of the learning environment for prospective teachers when they were in professional studies lectures at the university.

The focus of the observations was on the lecturer's performance, how the lecturer interacted with the students and how he or she managed the learning in the session. The lecturer was informed about the observation and so had a full explanation of the purpose of the observation. Informing the students about the purpose of the observation was left up to the lecturer being observed. None of the lecturers informed the students unless the students expressly asked. The observer merged into the student group of 100+ in the lectures, which were about 45 minutes in length. In reflecting on the observation approach, two issues arise. If the research was undertaken again it would probably be more appropriate for the students to have been informed of the researcher's purpose as a matter of ethics. However, the different cultural context has to be recognized. There was no expectation that the students needed to be informed beforehand although there was no problem discussing the purpose of the visit when and if they sought clarification.

The method of observation used was to record as much as possible in five-minute interval periods of what actually happens in the learning environment. The method was chosen after a pilot observation study at Exeter University, where a number of methods were tried. It was found that the five-minute interval recording of events etc. gave the richest descriptions of practice. After having undertaken a number of these in England, the researcher felt competent to do the same in Egypt. However, before doing the main study one or two pilot observations in Egypt were undertaken so that some issues that had not emerged in the English context could be taken into consideration. The events, activities, teacher's talking and dialogue between teacher and students and between students and students were recorded in order to provide a written description of the teaching session. A copy of any material handed out by the teacher to the students was collected. As it was physically impossible to record everything that happened during the teaching period, an audiotape recorder was used to record the lecturer's talk and the student responses. This had the purpose of providing more reliable data.

This observation was used with six pedagogical educators, each for three sessions to produce 18 observations. The observation sheet had four parts.

Part 1: Background information
Teacher's name:
Student's grade:
Subject:
Date:
Title:
Place:

Part 2: Physical environment

The place:	(lecture hall, laboratory)
Furniture:	(fixed, not fixed)
Number of students:	
Gender of students:	
Age of students:	
Teaching media:	microcomputers, overhead projector, television, video, blackboard, coloured chalk, microscope, others
Teaching resources:	books, equipment, non-teaching staff, ICT
Activity organization:	individual, small groups (2/3), large groups (more than 3)
Adequacy of materials:	more, equal, less, much less, no materials
Adequacy of instruments:	more, equal, less, much less, no materials
Map of the class:	

Part 3: Five-minute schedule

0–5 min	5–10 min	10–15 min	15–20 min	20–25 min

25–30 min	30–35 min	35–40 min	40–45 min	45–50 min

Part 4

(a) Teacher interview

It was a specific interview for specific data. The purpose was to find out the teacher's thinking that lay behind the specific teaching session, e.g. 'Why did you do that?' (different aspects of the session). This will provide the researcher with good understanding of several aspects of teaching and interpret and clarify the emerged issues in observation.

(b) Student interview

The purpose was to find out students' views about specific sessions, and to discuss all aspects of teacher teaching, such as the most useful things to them, the strengths and the weakness of the sessions (a neutral attitude towards the teacher teaching was shown by starting with the question, 'Was it an interesting session? How? Why?' and so on). The student sample was a group of students with different abilities, selected by the lecturer to comment on and discuss the lesson. The lecturer was asked to select the students because the lecturer could select students of different abilities. Such information was not available to the researcher. It might be considered a weakness of the design to allow the lecturer to choose the students to talk to the researcher. However, in the climate of the university, it was the only way forward.

Example 3 Jean's account of data collecting through observation of a group in action

This more extensive account exemplifies:

- a researcher's rationale for undertaking observation;
- awareness of the culture;
- the devising of strategies to separate two distinct roles of involvement with the project;
- sensitivity to actors in the setting;
- strategies in the data collection to generate a feeling of trustworthiness in the process.

Background

This research is being conducted in five schools in three local authorities. The schools cover a variety of contexts. They are an inner-city community college (education action zone), a rural community college, an urban primary school, an inner-city primary school and a rural primary school.

The schools in the research study are part of a larger cohort involving 15 schools in a pilot project to explore and develop strategies for promoting more effective home, school and community partnership. All the head-teachers or principals of the participating schools were invited to form action teams consisting of parents, governors, teachers, special needs co-ordinators, community members, family education/community education workers and/or anyone else who might wish to further the aim of the project in their school community.

The action teams are parent-led and the nature of the projects undertaken has been decided by each action team. Teams were all given information and advice to assist with their choice of projects from the parent teacher association project coordinators. The support materials offered to teams covered six areas of involvement: parenting, learning, communicating, collaborating with the community, consultation and decision-making, and volunteering. Within these six areas, teams were given a range of 170 suggestions to support their choice of project work. The teams were encouraged to choose projects that would complement work already under way at the school or in the local community and they could, if they wished, decide to try alternative approaches and disregard the suggestions.

The Investors in Parents project offers teachers and parents the opportunity to work more closely in a mutually supportive environment and it offers me, as researcher, an opportunity to investigate underlying attitudes of parents and teachers who are working together in an unusually parent-led, teacher-supported, project.

Methodology

The methodology I employed had to take into consideration the fact that I was the director of the initiative Investors in People. I am not a professional educator in any capacity. I do not have a teaching certificate and have never held any post in educational administration. All the work I am engaged in is voluntary. My interest is as a parent, and not as an educational professional. With both my personal experience of parenting children in a variety of school environments and my knowledge of other parents' experiences of the education system, I developed the concept of the Investors in Parents pilot project to support schools and families wishing to explore the potential of closer partnership working. The emphasis from the beginning was on parent leadership to support schools, rather than teacher-directed projects. I became interested in studying aspects of the project in a more systematic way, which led to my registering for a research degree to explore the area I found fascinating, namely parent–teacher attitudes and their affect on working relationships.

This research is less concerned with outcomes of the projects undertaken by the action teams than with illuminating the way in which parents and teachers work as individuals or team members in this unusual construct of a parent-led, teacher-participating team within a school.

In order to gather information which would reveal attitudes of parents and teachers that underlie the superficial strata of their interactions and conversations, I needed to develop a tool which would be capable of unpicking what is said, to reveal what is meant. I decided to use observation in the first instance to gather data on behaviour of team members at a meeting. This data would be coded in such a way as to reveal the group dynamics at work in the action teams, as well as the content of discussions in the meeting.

It was important for me to think in a positive and constructive way about my dual role as project director/researcher. My knowledge of the action teams as project director means that I am more acutely aware, during my visits as researcher, of the 'bigger picture' with regard to the practical challenges facing the teams in the project work, as well as the personal challenges facing some of the team members. As project director I have also been made aware of factors which would not have been revealed to me during my observations as researcher, and many of these factors are inevitably concerned with attitudes of other team members and their relationship with the school or parents. I am aware that the very specific sense in which information is given to me as project director will inform my observations as researcher. Therefore, by the time I arrived at the point of observing the action teams in my role of researcher, there was a real danger that my personal interaction as project director with the team individuals might adversely affect my interpretation of the data collected. I needed to develop strategies to separate out my interpretation of the situation prior to systematic data collection, so that I could make sure I benefited from the process of data collecting. Otherwise, why bother to collect information painstakingly if I had already decided what I was going to find! I did feel it was helpful to include some of the background I have gleaned in my role as project director. This personal knowledge would help me. I believe that to disregard this information would have impoverished the ultimate interpretation of the situation. The strategy I employed, in order to separate the background information that I have gathered as project director, which adds conceptual context to the observations, from the data collected by the researcher during the observations, was to use analytic memos and researcher's notes to record background information gathered prior to the meeting, as well as other information which complements the observation transcript.

The transcript itself is as purely descriptive as I could possibly make it.

It is a verbatim recording of the meetings observed and, together with observed actions of the team members, their seating arrangements and notes on the general environment, makes up the raw data and reads as a script for a stage play. Thus, as far as is achievable, I have separated the researcher's factual observation from the broader context of the action team activities. This offers the added value of using the analytic memo and researcher's notes to place the meeting in context.

The data in my analytic memos contain my thoughts, ideas and initial theories about the situations under study. This is a useful record for me. I have gained experience by working with parents and teachers both inside and outside the Investors in Parents project, which naturally impacts on my thinking. The analytic memos and researcher's notes serve very well as a reference point, made at the time of the observation and which will be confirmed, or otherwise, by the subsequent analysis of the transcript data. Thus, I can put the transcript data with my recorded analytic memo and researcher's notes and in so doing illustrate the difference between my intuitive feelings about the way that individuals in the action teams are working (recorded in the memos and notes), and the reality as illuminated (contained within the transcription).

Observation practice

Before conducting the observation I wrote formally to each action team chair asking whether they would raise this matter at their next action team meeting. I explained that the teams, the schools and any individuals would not be identified in the research and that unless all members of the team were willing to be recorded, I would not wish to attend the meeting as researcher. (Although I would attend and support the team in my role as project director, of course, on other occasions.) I explained that I would be following up the observation with interviews and asked whether the principal/headteacher and chair would be willing to participate. All five teams agreed to my request to tape an observation and the heads and chairs agreed to follow-up interviews.

I arrived at meetings early to set up my tape recorder which was large and red, making it highly visible, and placed where everyone could see it, but not necessarily in the centre of the table in all cases.

Before the meeting began, I asked to address the meeting for two minutes and explained that I was not there to act as project director on this occasion and could not participate in discussion. However, burning issues could be put on one side and I would answer questions at the end of the meeting. As the teams were aware that my role was non-participatory before I arrived at the meeting, the teams did not have many questions for me and were in most part able to conduct the meeting without any reference to me after the tape ended.

I asked at the start of the meeting, once again, whether there were any objections to my recording or from team members in being part of the research, and in every case there were no questions or objections. I set the 90-minute tape running at that point and made notes about the seating arrangements and where people had chosen to sit, body language, reactions to one another's presence and contributions to discussions. Before and after the meeting members of the teams came to me with comments. Sometimes these were noted by me after the meeting and recorded in the analytic memo, especially if they were concerned with conduct of other members during the meeting or attitudes which manifest themselves and which I thought might be relevant. All comments, including 'Ehms' and 'Aahs', hesitations and repetitions, were transcribed in case they may be significant.

Ask, listen, record: interviewing

The research literature is replete with advice and examples of interviewing practice. There are many ways of capturing the meanings and intentions of actors. What this section of the chapter sets out to do is to inform the reader of the particular way that I have developed interviewing as a technique both to collect data and, as described in the next chapter, to analyse it in a way that puts the research design and principles of researcher practice into action. I have employed this form of interviewing in all the research studies mentioned in this book.

I concur with the definition of the research interview offered by Cannell and Kahn (1968), who see it as 'a two-person conversation initiated by the interviewer for the specific purpose of obtaining research-relevant information'. I mention this definition in particular because I like the notion of a conversation, while accepting that it is a particular kind of conversation, not completely free flowing but focused by me, as researcher, on content that is oriented around the research brief.

The interview schedules that I devise for my research are most frequently designed to elicit descriptive and explanatory information that presents a picture of the interviewee's interpretation of the situation under study. Cohen and Manion (1980) suggest that there are four kinds of interview that are specifically used as research tools: the structured interview, the unstructured interview, the non-directive interview and the focused interview. To set my interview format and intention within the literature on research interviews it is worth quoting how Cohen and Manion (1980: 309–10) describe these four kinds of interview:

> The structured interview is one in which the content and procedures are organised in advance. This means that the sequence and wording of the questions are determined by means of a schedule and the interviewer is

> left little freedom to make modifications. Where some leeway is granted him, it too is specified in advance. It is therefore characterised by being a *closed* situation. In contrast to it in this respect, the unstructured interview is an *open* situation having greater flexibility and freedom . . .
>
> The non-directive interview as a research technique derives from the therapeutic or psychiatric interview. The principle features of it are the minimal direction or control exhibited by the interviewer and the freedom the respondent has to express his subjective feelings and as spontaneously as he chooses or is able.
>
> The need to introduce rather more interviewer control into the non-directive situation led to the development of the focused interview. The distinctive feature of this type is that it focuses on a respondent's subjective responses to a known situation in which he is involved and which has been analysed by the interviewer prior to the interview.

As with any description of types, the reality for each researcher is a mixture of types. I would call my interview format semi-structured and, as you will see from the example below, it contains elements from all the above in my own particular cocktail! A number of open questions are devised as a result of seeking to find a useful way to elicit responses to the research question. However, within each open-ended question there is information that I would dearly like to pick up on in all the interviews. These can be found in the schedule under the heading of 'pick ups'. It is structured like this so that I can trigger myself to note that if the interviewee does not offer information about these things in response to the open question, further subsidiary questions would need to be asked. This format has a number of benefits. First, it keeps the conversation free-flowing and I am able to judge the appropriate time to ask the subsidiary question in a manner that keys into the style of the conversation. Second, it ensures that equivalent information in the sense of the topics covered is collected in different interviews, thus fulfilling the research objectives. Third, it allows the interviewee the chance to expand on what she sees as a priority in her own situation. These are important data that it would not be possible to collect if I had structured the order of the questions and made them too specific and focused.

The style of the semi-structured qualitative interview

I would describe the main skill needed to conduct my semi-structured interview as that of *active listening*. It is active in the sense that the interviewer has to create an atmosphere that encourages the interviewee to talk freely and be clearly understood. If the interviewer is passive then there is no possibility of checking that what she has heard is, in fact, what the interviewee has been trying to say. Strategies have to be employed that give feedback and encourage concrete examples, explanations and expansion of what is initially said. This is necessary because an interpretive researcher wants rich data from her interviews in order to build up a picture of what is happening from the perspective of the interviewee. In practice active listening entails the listener in finding ways of reiterating what the talker is saying, e.g. 'If I understand you correctly you are saying . . .', or 'Let's go over what you have just said', 'I've made some notes, let me check whether I've got it right' and so on. The good active listener involves herself in the conversation in this way. Questions are asked that she genuinely wants to find out the answer to, and not the sort of questions that feed the kind of response that the interviewer would like to get. The active listener does not 'hog' the interview and does not give out her opinions. She constantly searches for the interviewees' meanings and practices.

Activity

Practise the 'listening' interview. Find a fellow professional to interview. Decide what it is you want to find out. For example, if you were interviewing a teacher you might want to find out (a) about the qualities and skills they think are necessary to be a good teacher and (b) what strengths and weaknesses they think they have in relation to the qualities and skills defined.

First set up a relaxed environment for the interview. Give the interviewee a time frame for the interview and try to stick to it; 30–40 minutes is often sufficient. Find a non-threatening way to introduce the idea of recording the interview to the respondent. Organize your interview questions and the way you will take notes during the interview.

The key approach as interviewer in the interview is to:

- hear what the interviewee has to say;
- ask neutral and non-threatening questions;
- ask them to provide examples of what they mean;
- feed back at regular intervals what they are saying in order to help them to be clear and to help you check out that you are understanding what they are saying.

Don't

- give advice or guidance during the interview;
- put your own interpretation on what they are saying during the interview;
- give anecdotes from your own experience.

Reflect

Listen to your tape of the interview and check out whether it was an active listening interview or an active talking interview on your part!

Example of a semi-structured interview schedule

I have included in Box 1 an example of an interview schedule devised for the research project entitled 'From policy to practice' which sought to answer the research question: 'What impact has the preparation for Key Stage 3 tests had on the working practices of heads of English departments in six comprehensive schools in England?'

The mechanics of conducting an interview

The interview schedule is structured to accommodate the taping of the interviews. A separate A4 sheet could be used for each question, with the question typed at the top of the page so that it is possible to note down key responses and subsidiary questions linked to the main question. Otherwise a sheet with the key questions on it and a notebook could be sufficient, depending on your individual style. However, even if I keep notes I always tape the interviews as well so that I have the richness of the data, the interviewees' words to work on and to analyse. I ask the interviewee at the beginning of the interview if they are happy about this. The tape recorder is small (but powerful), with standard tapes and a built-in microphone. Before arriving at the interview I make sure that the batteries are working and the tape is in place, with the title and a date spoken into the tape as well as a label on it. Then, if I get a positive response from the interviewee about using the tape recorder, I simply take it out of my bag and switch it on with a minimum of fuss. I carry spare batteries with me at all times, as well as spare tapes. Even so, writing main pieces of information that arise in the interview is worthwhile as it helps to identify key aspects of the interview that have struck you as you have been listening.

Conducting the interview: question order

Because the interview is semi-structured, unexpected areas of interest might arise and lead to other questions worth asking. It is also worth noting that although the questions are in a particular order in the schedule, it is important not to be a slave of the schedule order. A good qualitative researcher 'reads' the situation in which she is interviewing and may feel it is better to begin at a different place in the schedule or to phrase the question differently. What matters is for the interview to cover all the main areas you are seeking information about, so try to get it as naturalistically as possible. That means going 'with the flow' of the conversation and the context to make the respondent as relaxed and comfortable as possible. The finished interview is then transcribed and sent to the interviewee for confirmation. This is called *respondent validation* and gives the interviewee the opportunity to review what she or he has said, make corrections, add points and so on before the analysis is begun. The following chapter takes some of the interview data

Box 1 Interview schedule

Heads of department

Interview schedule

Name of teacher

Subject area

Name of school

Date of interview

Interview questions

Q1 How do you run your department?

Pick up:
- attitude to management theories
- relationship with department members
- role of HOD
- time in school/in the job
- practical examples of things that happen in the department

Q2 How would you describe the teaching that goes on in your subject area?

Pick up:
- teaching style
- use of resources
- classroom organization

Q3 Has the introduction of the NC resulted in any changes to that, however imperceptible or in the making?

Pick up:
- pupil–teacher relationships
- subject subcultural perspective
- other influences that have resulted in changes

Q4 Is the implementation of the NC having an effect on the curriculum content you have and the curriculum processes you use?

Pick up:
- general approach to content (set books/oral/choice)
- notions of quality of work

Q5 What effect will (have) assessment changes have (had) on classroom and management practices?

Pick up:
- Key Stage 3 proposals
- assessment impact on learning
- teacher assessment/moderation practices

Hilary A. Radnor
University of Exeter

collected from the study 'From policy to practice' and presents a model of the procedure for analysing the data.

Example of the author's data collecting practice

This chapter has sought to show the most common approaches to observing and interviewing when doing interpretive research in educational settings. Often research has to be conducted with constraints of time and money and pressures of other responsibilities put on individual researchers, many of whom are doing research alongside other work. These methods have proved to be both manageable and reliable for researchers, some of whom are completing PhD studies. As a way of concluding this chapter I have returned to my own PhD study (Radnor 1996) and produced an account of how I approached my fieldwork which integrated both observation and interviewing to collect the data. This account will also act as a bridge between this chapter and the next, as it not only indicates the data collecting process but also touches on the nature of data analysis and interpretation, which are the subject of Chapter 5.

Doing research at Parkview School

I gained access to the school through my job as lecturer in education at the university, supervising students on school experience. Discussions took place with the headteacher regarding the possibility of undertaking research in the school. I explained that I was interested in how the school managed to cope with the implementation of the new General Certificate of Secondary Education for all 16 year olds. Negotiations took place with the headteacher, his management team, which consisted of three deputy heads and a senior teacher, and five teachers who were heads of faculties and were known within the organizational structure as curriculum team leaders (CTLs).

The research design had two phases. Phase one involved the head and his team. The purpose here was to gain insight into the culture of the school management structure and particularly to gain a sense of the senior management perceptions of the staff's ability to manage curriculum change. The managers did not directly instruct their staff how to teach, but they did organize matters, so Schein's (1985: 6) interpretation of the meaning of culture is appropriate in this context:

> I would argue that the term 'culture' should be reserved for the deeper level of basic assumptions and beliefs that are shared by members of the organization, that operate unconsciously and that define in a basic 'taken for granted' fashion an organization's view of itself and its environment.

Visiting Parkview on a regular basis, I observed senior management team meetings, shadowed the head and deputies doing their everyday work and conducted semi-structured interviews with them. The interviews were transcribed and the transcriptions fed back to them for comment. That gave me a form of respondent validation. As far as the senior management were concerned I could have stopped there, but I decided to take the practice of respondent validation a step further. I was also aware that as a researcher I was part of the social process. I was interpreting their perceptions and making judgements as to their perspective on each other and the school staff in general. Hence I was keen to have my analysis open to scrutiny by them. So I prepared a report 'for their eyes only', which presented emergent themes that I identified that arose from the data collected. I asked for feedback, hoping that in seeing their independent views collated in this way, the participants would respond as a group and give me a sense of whether my interpretation resonated with them at all. Copies of the report were given to each member of the team, and I arranged to go into school to discuss the possibility of a group follow-up meeting. In writing about respondent validation Bloor (1978: 545) stated:

> The truth of analyses, their validity, is constituted by establishing some sort of correspondence between analysts and collectivity members' views of the world . . . One can establish a correspondence between the sociologists' and the members' view of the members' social world by exploring the extent to which members recognise, give assent to, the judgements of the sociologist.

Corresponding views were established between the individual members of the senior management team and myself. In my meeting with the head it transpired that the team had felt disconcerted by the inclusion of so many of their words that had illuminated rather graphically their views and opinions. Although not prepared to discuss the report as a group (for reasons to do with relationships among members of the group that the data revealed), all of them spoke to me independently. They recognized their words as reflected to them, but they were not particularly happy with what they saw!

The second phase of the fieldwork centred on the CTLs, the school's term for heads of department. As subject team leaders they were in the 'front line' with regard to the change to the GCSE. I concentrated on five CTLs, chosen because they were the subject leaders of subjects about which I had GCSE knowledge acquired in a previous project: English, science, mathematics, humanities, and craft, design and technology (Radnor 1987). During the time I was focusing on the senior team, I was also doing participant observation in the school more generally. I shadowed pupils in the relevant lessons, was party to departmental meetings of the focused subjects and held informal conversation with members of staff who worked for the CTLs. Therefore, by the time I started focusing in on the CTLs themselves I had sufficient knowledge of the way they worked to realize that a different approach to working in depth with them would be required. Bernstein's (1971) term – collection code – was recognizable in their working practices. 'Where knowledge is regulated through the collection code, the knowledge is organised and distributed through a series of well-insulated subject hierarchies' (Bernstein 1971: 61). The organizational consequences of this within the school structure meant that there was comparatively little communication and contact about educational and curriculum issues among the different CTLs. Their reference group was within the subject area, not across areas. Therefore, it seemed that I had to build a relationship with these teachers on an individual level and with each one independently of any other in a careful way before sharing my resultant analyses with them altogether. The first round of semi-structured interviews took place some time after the fieldwork had started and the teachers and I were already acquainted. These interviews were open-ended with the GCSE as the general focus. I asked them:

How are you coping with the change to GCSE?

What do you have to do to implement the change?

For what are you responsible?

What effect is the GCSE having on your teaching and the organization of the department?

The interview tapes were transcribed and the teachers given the opportunity to comment on them. I did an initial analysis of the material in which I categorized their issues and concerns. Many were shared, so I decided to follow up these interviews with a further one for each CTL, organized around a series of questions that grew out of the analysis of the first round. Consequently, although the questions were still open-ended they were more focused. In looking at the two sets of questions, the difference is perceptible and gives an indication of the kind of information gleaned from the analysis of the first round of interviews. I asked them:

Do you see yourself as managing other adults or working with them to deliver the curriculum?

Do you use the term deliver the curriculum? Is there another term you would rather use?

Would you change the curriculum if you had the option not to?

Do you feel in control of everything? Anything?

What do you feel is legitimately your responsibility in implementing curriculum changes?

I analysed these data and constructed my interpretive account by generating conceptual categories of their perspectives on working in that institution and managing curriculum change. I had a final interview with each CTL, and in that interview presented them with the conceptual categories that I had generated from the data and asked them if they recognized them as being a reflection of their experience. They all did and offered examples to illustrate their understanding of my interpretation. The next chapter discusses in more detail this process of analysing data to generate conceptual categories which then form the basis for interpreting and theorizing.

5 | Analysis and interpretation

Chapter 4 details the data collection process of observing and interviewing in a way that is concomitant with the interpretive approach. This chapter offers a technique for analysing the data with an example of practice. It also offers a way to develop from the analysis to interpretation. It may seem a contradiction to expound one particular technique of analysis considering the perspective on interpretivism advocated in this book so far. However, it is important not to equate the offering of a systematic approach to the data for the purpose of analysis with the idea of one correct method designed to elicit the only possible interpretation from the data collected. My theoretical approach to interpretivism in Chapter 2 presented my vision of people in society as active agents participating in a changing world of interaction within structural conditions. Such a stance recognizes the researcher as active constructor of meaning in coming to her or his definition of the situation under study. Hence there is a need to support the right of the interpretive researcher to make sense of their data and to justify their interpretation to the community. However, as a teacher as well as a researcher I found myself in a position where researchers were coming to me with their data, and saying, 'I have all this data, what do I do with it, how do I begin to analyse it?' Over a period of years this approach has emerged, my response to managing my own data and helping others to manage theirs. The approach is based on the notion of helping to order the data so that it is possible for the researcher to consider them clearly. It advises a consistent, thoughtful ordering (not a mechanistic one), so as to encourage rigour without rigidity, leading to the researcher being able to give an account of their interpretation as a result of laying out the data in a way that stimulates careful analysis.

The data collected from a semi-structured interview, as described in Chapter 4, are used here to illustrate the technique. However, the technique holds good for data collected from more structured interviews, group discussions/meetings that have been taped and transcribed or observation data that have been carefully recorded describing activities, behaviour and talk of the participants. Jean's account of her data collecting from the action teams is a good example of this. In discussing what she will do with the data collected, she writes:

> All five observations, recorded on audio tape and transcribed verbatim with supporting analytic memos and researcher's notes, will be coded for content and group dynamics. The data will be compared one team with another to find common themes and idiosyncrasies. After thorough analysis of the data, semi structured interviews will be conducted with selected action team members. Questions for the interviews will be used to verify or tease out underlying attitudes which are made apparent during the data analysis. So, the observations are not an end in themselves. They are a tool used to verify, or otherwise, data gathered at the second stage, the semi structured interview. The observation coding is designed to reduce the data to categorical statements which are capable of revealing attitudes which can then be verified or otherwise by data gathered at the next stage. The semi-structured interviews will also be recorded, transcribed, coded and analysed. This data will be compared with the observation data in an endeavour to illuminate underlying attitudes of parents and teachers to partnership working.
>
> (Personal correspondence to supervisor, November 2000)

Jean intends to use the analysis method described in this chapter. The first part of the chapter presents the analysis technique through presenting a stage by stage procedure with an exercise designed for you to practise the approach with data from the project 'From policy to practice'. This is followed by an example of the process as used by one of my research students, Mamoon Al-Momeni, in his PhD study on teacher perceptions of their mandatory in-service course. It is a useful example because he uses a more structured interview, but the technique still holds good. The final part of the chapter discusses the process of moving on from analysis to interpretation using as illustration, once again, 'From policy to practice'.

Analysis technique using the semi-structured qualitative interview

Analysing a qualitative interview involves close examination of the information you have collected in order to find an answer to your research question. When you engage in this process you arrive at descriptions of the interviewees' attitudes, values and beliefs, and their perceptions of their practices. From these series of descriptions an interpretation is provided based on the evidence that has been systematically organized. This gives insight into the situation under study, enabling you to understand it better. Following the analysis you go one stage further and interpret the findings. This should lead to the generation of a theoretical explanation through recognition of patterns and relationships between the different kinds of phenomena that have been illuminated by the analysis.

Preparing your data for analysis

Before going into the analysis proper it is first necessary to prepare the data for analysis. The preliminary work I call 'topic ordering' and I describe it thus.

Preparation for the analysis process begins when you are designing your research. By that I mean the way you will analyse has been thought through from the moment you have decided on how you will collect the data. The type of questions you ask of your respondents or the focus of your observations during your fieldwork form the framework from which your analysis will be generated. I call preparation for analysis 'topic ordering' because it is like you going into a room with your papers strewn all around in no particular order, determined to put them into some kind of order – to sort and classify them. You know what topics these papers cover because they are your papers and you are familiar with them, so you arrive in the room with some boxes. The first step is to get all the papers that are connected in some kind of way into the same box. It is a breaking down job so you begin by separating the papers out into broad areas that are encompassing. You decide, in the first instance, to separate out personal documents from professional documents. That gets all the papers off the floor and into a box. You then take the personal box and having scanned them for topics you decide to divide them further into three boxes entitled correspondence with friends, household and garden. You then do the same with your professional box. Are you beginning to get the picture?

You need some kind of structure in which you can view your data and although you are unclear what you have found out until you analyse your data (otherwise what would have been the point of collecting all those data!), you are clearer about the topics you covered in collecting your data. *So use these topics as the basis of your sorting system and work from there.*

After the topic ordering process described above the procedure for organizing the qualitative interview data for analysing a taped transcript becomes an inductive one. In other words, you do not start with ready made categories within the main topics but allow them to emerge from the data as you become more and more familiar with the contents. This means reading the taped transcripts a number of times: the expression is 'staying close to the data'. My procedure is based on the assumption that there will be more than one interview, so a procedure is needed to tabulate the responses that enables the researcher to analyse systematically.

Although this procedure is useful with one or more interviews, perhaps to try out the approach it would be helpful to begin by practising with one

Activity

This activity concentrates on interview data. Take your own interview data and write down the topics covered. If you are using my data look at the open-ended questions in the interview schedule (Chapter 4) that are prompts for answers and identify the major topics from them.

It is worth noting that if you have thought hard about your research brief you will have shaped your interview schedule in such a way as to cover the main topic areas to which you want a response. These topic areas will give you the main sorting boxes into which to drop your data pieces. A data piece is a section of dialogue that is about that topic. In some data pieces, the respondent may cover more than one topic, so it would appear in both boxes. *Data pieces do not have to be mutually exclusive.*

interview. Working from a copy of a taped transcript will give you the data base. You could use either an interview you have conducted yourself or the material offered here.

A step-by-step guide to analysis

There are six steps to this technique:

1 Topic ordering.
2 Constructing categories.
3 Reading for content.
4 Completing the coded sheets.
5 Generating coded transcripts.
6 Analysis to interpreting the data.

Step 1 Topic ordering

List topics that appear on reading the whole text. The original questions give access to some of the topics. From the interview schedule in Chapter 4 you can see that the topics in the interview are oriented around teaching, assessment, management and so on. However, it is important to read the interviews carefully to make sure you draw out any further topics from the text: that is, those topics embedded implicitly in the responses as well as topics that are explicitly stated through the interview schedule. Once happy with the topics listed, use clean sheets of A4 for each topic. You can do this either on paper or on the word processor.

Each topic has its own sheet of A4 . The topic name and an abbreviation (identifiable code) is put at the top of the page, e.g.

Topic: Assessment
Code: ASS

You are now ready to set up the data analysis sheets.

Step 2 Constructing categories

Once the topics have been identified, the categories within each topic are constructed. The topic areas are 'holding forms' that help you to access the data in a manageable way and provide a structure through which categories are constructed that emerge from reading the data carefully.

Categories may be of different kinds. Two of the most common kinds are:

- those that are *explicit* in the data, e.g. reasons given for liking a particular kind of experience, managing in a particular way, using a particular teaching material;
- those that are *implicit* in the data and so are constructed by the researcher, e.g. bringing together responses to do with attitudes to change, ideological perspectives, relationships within teaching teams.

Read the transcripts again and write sub-headings to each topic. These sub-headings are your categories. Areas of interest, issues and concerns discussed in the interview can generate these. Each A4 sheet starts to fill up, e.g.

Topic: Assessment
Code: ASS
1 ideological perspective
2 expected practice pre-NC (National Curriculum)
3 expected practice post-NC
4 attitude to external assessment/SATS (standard assessment tests)
5 attitude to teacher assessment
6 actual practice

Step 3 Reading for content

We are now ready to code *content* to topic categories by going through the text and circling/marking the main quotes. The A4 sheets set-up means that the quotes do not, at this stage, need to be cut and pasted, simply marked and coded so that they can be found again. This is done as follows. The code name is written next to the text and the category number that describes the text put next to it. However, just in case there is another chunk of data that can go into that category from the interview (or another interview if you have more than one) the piece of text is also given a letter

(A–Z) to differentiate it from other pieces of text. This means we are able to locate the quote on the original text quickly. For example, if the text has a statement about teacher attitude to assessment then that part of the text will be highlighted, circled, underlined (whichever you prefer) and in the margin ASS 6A will be written – ASS is the code, 6 is the category heading and A denotes that it is the first quote under that category found (see the extract of interview that follows).

> **Activity**
>
> Take the extract of the interview given below and read it carefully. Note the data chunks and how they have been picked out to be categorized under the topic 'Assessment'. Do you agree with the data chosen? Would you have chosen any others to go in these categories? You may well find differences and if so you can ask yourself why. Interpretive analysis is inductive. It would be unusual for each researcher to read the text in exactly the same way. The key notion here is credibility. So if you and I don't agree, check to see if we both pass the credibility test.

An extract of a coded transcript of the interview with DB with assessment codes

Interview with DB, Head of English City School, 23 September 1992 (first interview).

H: *Can we start with your reaction to the English developments in the National Curriculum.*

D: Most people I know, the people I grew up with as a teacher, felt the Cox report vindicated the best of the good practice that we had all learnt you know through going to the English Centre and working with colleagues – it was wonderful. When this guy who had been one of the authors of the Black Papers suddenly said well actually this is good practice we felt great. The actual recording of the assessment side of things has been hard to take on but I don't mind that really because we could still carry on teaching in exactly the right sort of ways. What we are depressed about is the current turn of events, the way things have been moving. People have been predicting but we have kind of known, really, what we were in for but the grim reality of it is hitting us very very hard and very swiftly because we are not having time to think. It is all very brutal. What we are trying to do, what good English teachers are trying to do is trying to retain the best of all those things we believe are right about

English teaching in the face of pressure to narrow everything and streamline it and that obviously makes me and everybody else I know who are any good at it feel very sad. And I think people will leave, will give it up literally as a bad job. ASS 1A

H: What do you see as the most brutal?

D: OK. Case in point the way in which the assessment at Key Stage 3 is coming into schools now. We have known that there would be assessment for our year 9 students in the first week of June 1993. We learnt when it was going to be. I think, last term. We are now, this week, getting into schools details of what they are going to be assessed on and it is highly prescriptive particularly in literature where we are suddenly told it has got to be one of these three Shakespeare texts for the bright kids. The brighter children. Yeah OK we can throw a quick course together on *Midsummer Night's Dream* but that is not how we work. It is not the best way of working. It is not that we aren't doing Shakespeare with Year 9. I have been doing Shakespeare with young kids for years but it is suddenly we are being told it has to be one of these three and to get a course together quickly. It is not the way we work. It doesn't produce good methods or good content and it angers us basically.

H: So in fact you are going to have to ditch what you have been doing, what you have discussed, negotiated and so on?

D: Yes. Last year I evolved, I think, a very good unit of work on *The Tempest* which I used with Year 9 students. It got them well into the text, they got into paraphrasing you know. I linked up with the drama teacher and she did stuff on it in drama. There was a lot of textual work involved where really kids who had never dreamt they could handle Shakespeare could work with the language. It was wonderful and I planned to do it this year – I can't. It is not one of the prescribed texts. But I haven't got the time to evolve a similar unit of work with one of those prescribed texts. *Not* to my satisfaction anyway and that is why I feel angry about it. They are going to test these children without giving us the time to give them quality work to lead up to it. ASS 4A I know that the fact is the less able kids are entered for a different tier and they don't have to do Shakespeare but that is not the way we work. When we teach we teach Shakespeare to all of them and of course the road they want us to go down is to stream them – let's stream them out, let's band them, let's get back into bright kids doing Shakespeare and not so bright doing something else . . .

H: They are asking you to differentiate the kids into these bands and giving you prescribed texts for all the different bands/tiers?

D: It is only the top two tiers that have to answer a question on

Shakespeare in the exam and the other tier they can answer a question on another text which we choose from a prescribed list. We haven't got that list yet but we have been told that it will be a list that takes into consideration what is in their stock cupboards, so we can be fairly sure that it will be predictable things – but nevertheless fancy not knowing now nearly in October. Everything is supposed to be happening in November. Everything is coming in November. We have got to get agreement trials going. I don't even know if we've got to mark the papers.

ASS 3A

H: You are – they can't afford to do anything else. You are given a mark scheme.

D: Right, in which case I have got to get my faculty trained into agreeing levels.

H: I think they will give you quite a tight mark scheme for the papers and then you are audited through the exam boards.

D: It is really hard to sell this. You asked me about teaching English and how I feel about it. One of the things I have always felt about myself. I am an enthusiastic teacher of English. I still love teaching. I still find what I do in the classroom is the most rewarding part of the job I do and I have always felt I could enthuse other people but I am up against it now for the hard facts of what our life has become in terms of assessing recording and now these SATs and all of that which means the younger teachers are harder to hold because they are saying – yeah that is all very well having these brilliant ideas for teaching this or that but I haven't time for this or time for that – and it is very very difficult and in the end I fear that we will end up with good people leaving because they just see the gloom of it all and us being left with people who play into the hands of those that want to streamline English. It is easier to teach grammar exercises from a text than it is to devise imaginative programmes of work.

H: Do you feel there is a tendency for the members of the faculty to move in that direction?

D: Yes. I would say that against their better nature and against everything they want for themselves in their teaching lives – ultimately there is a core inside them that says I have a life to live and I can't cope with all of this and therefore things have to be thrown away. At the faculty meeting tonight I had asked people to come with units of work prepared for the Key Stage 3 curriculum we've worked on together and we have been doing this since June and yet when the meeting came together in the end they weren't there on the table and the answer that is given to me is well I have just been under so much pressure, I have got to do this, I have got to do that and it is very hard to know how to handle that. Part of me reacts quite angrily and says 'you've had ages to do this, we are all busy, we are all under pressure you should have done it' and another part of me feels . . . well I understand how it has happened because I am not doing things I wish I were doing because I've been sidetracked.

H: Has the NC found you being more controlling as HOD?

D: I think my personal situation – I think this is relevant – when I came into Viewside as head of department, because I had been out in teacher training and things. When I was appointed I inherited a situation in which (a) the personnel in the faculty had been very unhappy and at odds with the head of faculty and therefore nothing of any value had been produced in a coherent collaborative way forever it seemed, and (b) I was under strict instructions in inverted commas to drag together as quickly as possible a Key Stage 3 curriculum and I had two terms really in which I had to get that done and we made a lot of progress and I didn't mind controlling that side of things but ultimately I have to leave control in the hands of the people who are devising the materials. I can't put together every booklet myself and now I am up against it because I am at a point where we have planned things we have agreed, things we have got a structure. We like it, it works, we think it is going to be great but where are the materials? Where is the flesh to put on the bones? The climate we are in at the moment makes it easy for people to say I haven't had the time.

H: So what in fact are you teaching?

D: Well we have worked out a series of units for each of the three Years 7 to 9 and they are progressive, they go through the years so you are building on the narrative skills, you are building on their ability to investigate poetry or whatever, you are building on their media education skills through the three years. We have all agreed that and think it is a healthy way to look at the curriculum. It doesn't actually mean that everyone is teaching this at this time but I should be able at the end of a year to assume that these NC targets have been met if everyone has done those units of work because the units in themselves should fulfil the programmes of study, yes. And that is what people are supposed to be doing now.

H: So what are they doing, what are they working on?

D: We have got some in place already but we can't hop from half term to half term. We have got to feel secure that those things are in place for the term and the term after that and that is what I am finding hard to get from people because ultimately as I have said they are too pressured either as form tutors or in their home lives or by Key Stage 4 and all of that to give it the time it needs and as I say part of me can understand and sympathize but the head of faculty in me wants to thump the table, come on we agreed, get on with it.

H: *How many have you in the faculty now?*

D: There are six of us full-time and two people that help from other faculties and I have currently got an agency teacher who is teaching a sixth form, GCSE mature class because we had a huge group of 56 on roll. We have got a strict contract going with the sixth form students that they have to meet or they are thrown off the course so we envisage that group maybe becoming one by half term but she is here with us until then. Actually they are all hanging in there at the moment so I don't know what we will do then. If we have got them and they are working I am very pleased but we are not resourced for them at the moment. [Sixth form numbers 160 at the moment.]

H: *So you envisage a resource bank of all these units that people can use whenever they like. But does that have an effect on your resources when everyone wants to do the same thing at the same time?*

D: Well not really because most of the booklets are guidance for teachers booklets, they are not packs of things that need massive duplicating – it is ways of approaching something.

H: *There are enough books and materials around for groups to work on the same thing?*

D: The idea is that if we have got enough units worked out it should always be possible to go and do something else if the materials you need to work with of a particular unit are overused.

H: *So it should be possible for individuals to negotiate the order without you having to timetable it?*

D: Oh yes. I mean that is more of a problem at Key Stage 4. The timetable of resources and the sharing of resources is much more difficult at Key Stage 4 but I think in the Years 7 to 9 it should not be a problem. We have still got a fairly healthy stock cupboard that can serve the units that we are devising. We don't need to go and buy masses and masses of things but it is something that we are well aware could change very dramatically.

H: *So the assessment thing – the moving back to tests. Have you been doing teacher assessment – the recording?*

D: With Years 8 and 9 they were assessed all last year when they were Years 7 and 8 and what it amounted to was a combination of things. We had to have moderation meetings to discuss levels and what level 3 was and what level 4 was. We certainly didn't do it thoroughly because again in two terms there wasn't time to do it thoroughly but nevertheless we had moderation meetings like you would have GCSE moderation meetings and we brought materials

ASS 5A

in and looked at them and came to a consensus. After that people were asked to take each of their classes and mark on a levels grid when they felt a kid had achieved a particular level on one of the attainment strands and in addition to that they had self-assessment sheets for the children to fill in with the teachers on reading, writing, speaking and listening. So every child in the current Years 8 and 9 should have a folder which contains those things I have described and samples of their work to justify, illustrate the level given by the teacher. We keep these records – there is a storage problem there. Of course with Year 7 we are starting them now.

H: *In terms of the moderation of levels – do you do that internally or do you have any links with other schools?*

D: The first one is going to be on 30 November. It is a SATs INSET day for the whole of the borough and all the subjects are going to go off to their various inspectors and advisory teachers and spend the whole day looking at assessment at Key Stage 3. That is the time we are going to meet with other faculties in English and discuss practical approaches to the final assessment at the end of Year 9 but it will obviously involve continuous assessment in Years 7 and 8.

ASS 6A

H: *A decision has been made by the government that the NC tests [apart from Speaking and Listening and in some instances of presentation (AT4/5)] take precedence and are the recorded level?*

D: Oh, we know in the end. I think it is dreadful. We are being allowed to assess handwriting I think, presentation and speaking and listening but in reading and writing no matter how meticulous we keep our records and how in the end our opinion is justified, if it conflicts with the exam assessment it won't be taken into consideration. From the point of view of leading a faculty it gives you a hell of a job. On the one hand you are insisting that these pressured people have to keep these records and yet not disguising from them the fact that ultimately they are not taken into account at all. And so you are thrown back on talking about assessment in terms of being diagnostic and that we need to do it in order that we make sure our expectations for each child are right and you know all of that but ultimately they say, well?

ASS 5B

H: *Does it hold water?*

D: Does it hold water? I don't need to fill in a grid to tell you whether *x*, *y* or *z* is achieving his or her potential, I can tell you now. I mean it is all a big game.

H: *There is a feeling is there that it is an administrative function that you have to carry out?*

D: Yes, to satisfy the powers that be. On the other hand I am quite pleased to be in a position where I have to say to people I want to see records, I want to see assessment. I must say I am quite pleased

about that because I think it has been a failing in even good English
ASS faculties over the years I have been teaching that we depend so
5C much on a teacher's opinion and what a teacher carries around
what is in his/her head and when they go unless they write meticulous notes you have lost it all. So I am actually quite keen to have them assessed but it doesn't have to be done in this way. I could ask them to do something much more simple and less time consuming and get the same amount of information I need.

H: *How does it tie in with what you are being asked to do in English and a whole-school policy on assessment?*

D: Well I mean that is sort of pie in the sky. Everybody is talking about how we need to have a whole-school policy and there is a group in the school who are into raising achievement and all of that and we did do a pilot scheme last spring term where we all agreed to teach our Year 7 classes a unit of work in every subject, and before we set the unit we had to write down what we thought the kid's levels were and after the unit we had to write down what the students had achieved. It was all laudable and good and we have yet to sit round a table and discuss the findings. It is so hard to actually get this going because of everything else going on, appraisal Key Stage 4.

Step 4 Completing the coding sheets

When the transcript has been coded, take your prepared A4 coded sheet for each topic (as in step 2 above) and insert the appropriate codes in the correct places. A coded sheet is included in Box 2 to give you an example.

You will see why such a sheet is useful especially when there is more than one interview. Here there are three interviews – interviewees identified as C, D and A – and the sheet enables identification of the different chunks of data from each interview to be clearly visible on one sheet. This means I have a means of gaining a picture of the number of data chunks on each topic across the three interviews and a reference for finding them quickly in the original text. Note that D in the coded sheet is the D in the interview example in step 3.

Step 5 Generating coded transcripts

When the transcripts have been coded and the data sheet filled out the transcripts are photocopied if a computer is not used. This is very important because it is absolutely necessary *to keep a master copy intact at all times*. If a computer is not used you will proceed to cut and paste the data under categories. However, it is easier to do this with a word processor using the copy and paste functions. I say copy and paste rather than cut and paste so that I retain the intact copy of the whole interview in the computer as well. It is

Box 2 The HR A4 coded sheet of three interviews using the same interview schedule

Topic: Assessment
Code: ASS

Interview 1: C
Interview 2: D
Interview 3: A

1 Ideological perspective
D: a, C: a
2 Expected practice pre-NC
C: a
3 Expected practice with NC
A: a b c d, D: a, C: a b
4 Attitude to external assessment/SATS
A: a b c, D: a, C: a
5 Attitude to teacher assessment
A: a b c, D: a b c
6 Actual practice
A: a, D: a, C: a

not necessary to have a qualitative data package to get the benefit of computer assistance, although it is possible that an appropriate one might cut down the amount of time this stage takes. However, I have not yet found one appropriate to my needs.

Below you will see how I have reproduced the categorized data chunks of the topic 'Assessment' for that one interview in a master assessment file. When I analyse other interviews using the same categories I can add the other data chunks to this master assessment file. This gives me access to all data in these categories in the same place. Having chunks of data is important. They must make sense out of context or I have no way of going on to the next stage and interpreting them. The taking of data from the mass and their re-emergence under a category heading is what makes interpretation possible. In interpretive research it is not necessary for the data to be put into only one category. Data chunks can have information within them that could be categorized in more than one place. This happens because in abstracting the data chunk from the whole it needs to be able to stand on its own and make clear sense, and the section of text may incorporate management issues with assessment or teaching with assessment, for example. As these categories emerged from this interview data they generally proved relevant with regard to other interviews that followed the same semi-structured interview schedule. However, new categories may emerge from the data of other interviews because, as I mentioned in discussing the carrying out of interviews, there were opportunities for the interviewees to dwell on areas that were priorities for them.

An extract of a copy and paste from the transcript to a master assessment file

The assessment categories arising from the D interview extract were:

- ideological perspective;
- expected practice with NC;
- attitude to external assessments/SATs;
- attitude to teacher assessment;
- actual practice.

TOPIC: Assessment

Category: Ideological perspective
(text from transcript)

D: What we are trying to do, what good English teachers are trying to do is trying to retain the best of all those things we believe are right about English teaching in the face of pressure to narrow everything and streamline it and that obviously makes me and everybody else I know who are any good at it feel very sad. And I think people will leave, will give it up literally as a bad job. Case in point the way in which the assessment at Key Stage 3 is coming into schools now. We have known that there would be assessment for our Year 9 students in the first week of June 1993. We learnt when it was going to be, I think, last term. We are now, this week, getting into schools details of what they are going to be assessed on and it is highly prescriptive.

Category: Expected practice with NC
(text from transcript)

H: They are asking you to differentiate the kids into these bands and giving you prescribed texts for all the different bands/tiers.

D: It is only the top two tiers that have to answer a question on Shakespeare in the exam and the other tier they can answer a question on another text which we choose from a prescribed list. We haven't got that list yet but we have been told that it will be a list that takes into consideration what is in their stock cupboards, so we can be fairly sure that it will be predictable things – but nevertheless fancy not knowing now nearly in October. Everything is supposed to be happening in November, everything is coming in November. We have got to get agreement trials going. I don't even know if we've got to mark the papers.

H: *You are – they can't afford to do anything else. You are given a mark scheme.*

D: Right, in which case I have got to get my faculty trained into agreeing levels.

H: *I think they will give you quite a tight mark scheme for the papers and then you are audited through the exam boards.*

D: It is really hard to sell this.

Category: Attitude to external assessment/SATS
(text from transcript)

D: I haven't got the time to evolve a similar unit of work with one of those prescribed texts. *Not* to my satisfaction anyway and that is why I feel angry about it. They are going to test these children without giving us the time to give them quality work to lead up to it.

Category: Attitude to teacher assessment
(text from transcript)

H: *So the assessment thing – the moving back to tests. Have you been doing teacher assessment – the recording?*

D: With Years 8 and 9 they were assessed all last year when they were Years 7 and 8 and what it amounted to was a combination of things. We had to have moderation meetings to discuss levels and what level 3 was and what level 4 was. We certainly didn't do it thoroughly because again in two terms there wasn't time to do it thoroughly but nevertheless we had moderation meetings like you would have GCSE moderation meetings and we brought materials in and looked at them and came to a consensus. After that people were asked to take each of their classes and mark on a levels grid when they felt a kid had achieved a particular level on one of the attainment strands and in addition to that they had self-assessment sheets for the children to fill in with the teachers on reading, writing, speaking and listening. So every child in the current Years 8 and 9 should have a folder which contains those things I have described and samples of their work to justify, illustrate the level given by the teacher.

D: We are being allowed to assess handwriting I think, presentation and speaking and listening but in reading and writing no matter how meticulous we keep our records and how in the end our opinion is justified, if it conflicts with the exam assessment it won't be taken into consideration. From the point of view of leading a faculty it gives you a hell of a job. On the one hand you are insisting that these pressured people have to keep these records and yet not disguising from them the fact that ultimately they are not taken into account at all. And so you are thrown back on talking about assessment in terms of being diagnostic and that we need to do it in order that we make sure our expectations for each child are right and you know all of that but ultimately they say, well?

H: Does it hold water?

D: Does it hold water? I don't need to fill in a grid to tell you whether *x*, *y* or *z* is achieving his or her potential, I can tell you now. I mean it is all a big game.

H: There is a feeling is there that it is an administrative function that you have to carry out?

D: I am quite pleased to be in a position where I have to say to people I want to see records, I want to see assessment. I must say I am quite pleased about that because I think it has been a failing in even good English faculties over the years I have been teaching that we depend so much on a teacher's opinion and what a teacher carries around what is in his/her head and when they go unless they write meticulous notes you have lost it all. So I am actually quite keen to have them assessed but it doesn't have to be done in this way. I could ask them to do something much more simple and less time consuming and get the same amount of information I need.

Category: Actual practice
(text from transcript)

H: In terms of the moderation of levels – do you do that internally or do you have any links with other schools?

D: The first one is going to be on 30 November. It is a SATs INSET day for the whole of the borough and all the subjects are going to go off to their various inspectors and advisory teachers and spend the whole day looking at assessment at Key Stage 3. That is the time we are going to meet with other faculties in English and discuss practical approaches to the final assessment at the end of Year 9 but it will obviously also involve continuous assessment in Years 7 and 8.

An example of a PhD student's analysis process of interview data

This process of analysis has been undertaken by a number of research students, so before we discuss the move on to interpretation, what follows is an example of a student's use of the analysis procedure outlined here.

In his PhD study, which is researching perceptions of an in-service programme for fine arts teachers in Jordan, Mamoon first engaged in semi-structured interviews with a number of trainees. His approach to analysing

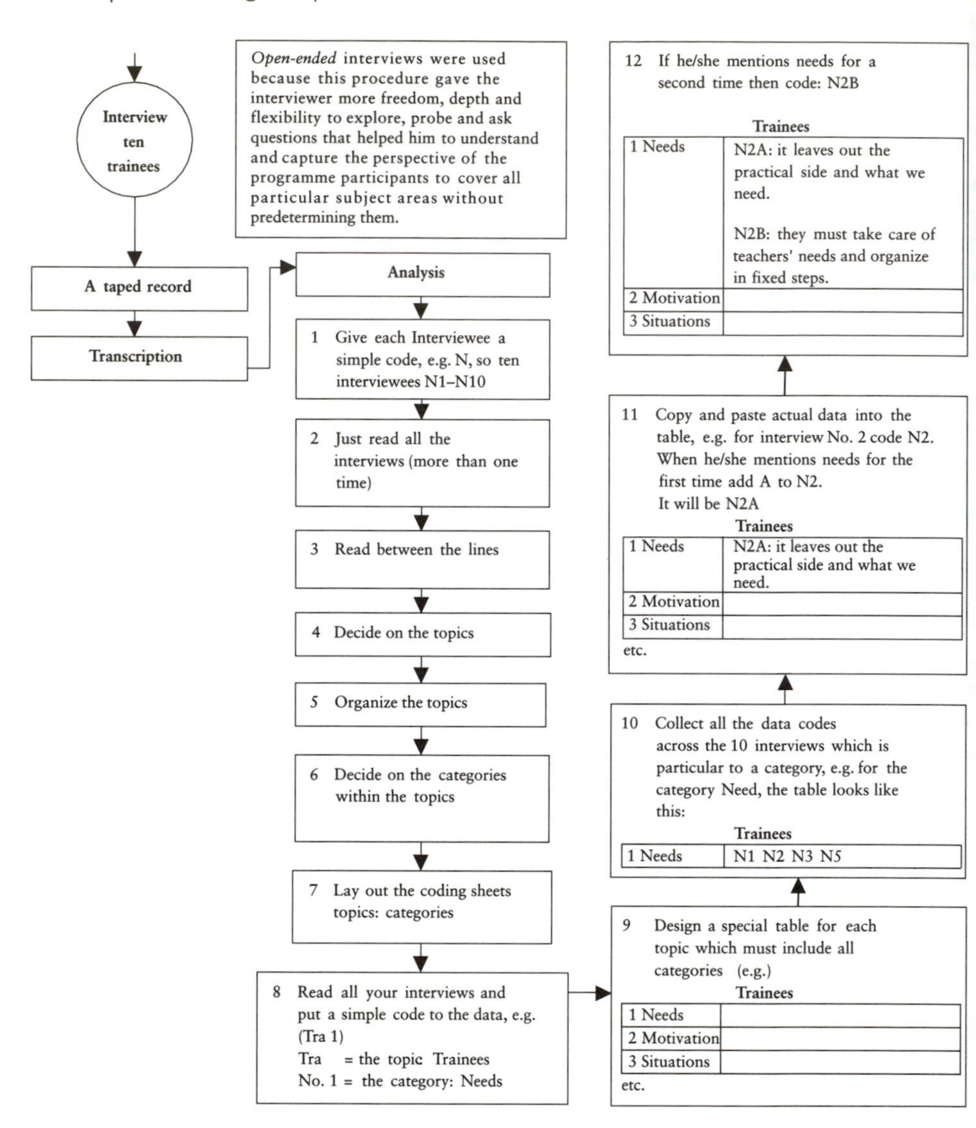

Figure 1 Mamoon's analysis process of trainees' perceptions of the current INSET programme

the data was modelled on that offered above. His analysis process is presented in diagrammatic form in Figure 1: 12 boxes describe 12 stages.

Figure 2 shows the topics and the categories in the topics generated by Mamoon in reading his data from interviews with the trainees. You can locate where this came in his analysis by looking at Figure 1, box 7.

The following extract from the interview transcript gives a flavour of his

Topic	Code	Categories	
Training design	TD	1	date
		2	time
		3	place
		4	facilities
		5	media
		6	structure
Course	C	1	aims
		2	planning
		3	organization
		4	management
		5	content
		6	skills covered
		7	methods
		8	materials
Professional development	PD	1	influence on the classroom
		2	influence on the trainees' personality
		3	usefulness to the classroom
		4	to the trainees personality
		5	effectiveness
		6	achievement
Evaluation of	E	1	weaknesses
		2	strengths
		3	evaluation methods
		4	troubles/problems
		5	importance of INSET in general
		6	importance of the current INSET programme
Trainer	Tr	1	qualifications/knowledge
		2	experiences
		3	teaching style/techniques
		4	behaviours
		5	ability to teach
		6	characters
		7	relationship
		8	motivations
		9	ten skills
Trainee	Tra	1	needs
		2	motivations
		3	situations
		4	relations
		5	feelings
		6	usefulness of the training
		7	expectations
		8	suggestions/recommendations

Figure 2 Trainee's perceptions of the current INSET programme: topics, codes and categories

process of descriptive analysis. His style of interviewing is moving more towards the structured than semi-structured. The first extract is uncoded and the second is the same extract coded. This is his version of undertaking what I call step 3: reading for content. In Figure 1, showing his analysis process, reading for content is numbered 8.

Activity

You have been given Mamoon's topics and categories in Figure 2. Below you have an extract that is not coded from an interview of the trainees. Look at the topics and categories and see if you can code this extract. You will find Mamoon's coded extract after this.

It is a useful example because it shows how it is possible to use the model advocated in this chapter with open-ended interview data, semi-structured interview data or structured interview data. It is also possible to use the method with group interviews. In fact, if you have words transcribed from interviews or observations when you record a meeting or a discussion, this method of analysis is possible.

Extract 1a from interview transcript: not coded

Q7: What is your role during the programme?

N5: As a trainee, I focus on the skills taught during classes, either application skills, or evaluation skills. Then I transfer them to classroom. I cooperate with the group members to produce a good job.

Q8: If I followed you through a typical day, what would I see you doing inside your classroom?

N5: Transferring most of the experiences I have been trained on. I prepare the necessary aids and tools in the fine art room. Then, I continue to apply the skills to ensure that my students master them.

Q9: How influential do you think INSET has been in causing change in your classroom?

N5: The programme has prepared me to perform new skills in the classroom.

Q10: What is the effect of the programme on your personality as a teacher?

N5: I admit the programme affected my personality as a teacher in the classroom positively. There is a difference in the classroom setting before and after the programme. Now I'm more flexible with my students.

Q11: Do you think the programme was effective? If yes, to what extent? If no, why?

N5: Yes, the programme was effective to some extent. It reinforced many things in my teaching, such as enquiry based learning.

Q12: How about trainers' performance?

N5: As far as their relationship with us is considered, they have been good, but it should be said that they were incompetent in fine arts skills training. They should have made use of the experience of the teachers in the group.

Extract 1b from interview transcript: coded

Q7: What is your role during the programme?
N5: As a trainee, I focus on the skills taught during classes (TRA6), either application skills or evaluation skills. Then I transfer them to classroom (PD3) I cooperate with the group members (TRA4) to produce a good job.
Q8: If I followed you through a typical day what would I see you doing inside your classroom?
N5: Transferring most of the experiences I have been trained on (TRA6). I prepare the necessary aids and tools in the fine art room. Then, I continue to apply the skills to ensure that my students master them. (PD1)
Q9: How influential do you think INSET has been in causing change in your classroom?
N5: The programme has prepared me to perform new skills in the classroom. (PD1)
Q10: What is the effect of the programme on your personality as a teacher?
N5: I admit the programme affected my personality as a teacher in the classroom positively (PD2). There is a difference in the classroom setting before and after the programme. Now I'm more flexible with my students.
Q11: Do you think the programme was effective? If yes, to what extent? If no, why?
Yes, the programme was effective to some extent. It reinforced many things in my teaching, such as enquiry based learning. (PD5)
Q12: How about trainers' performance?
N5: As far as their relationship with us is considered, they have been good (TR7), but it should be **said** that they were incompetent in fine arts skills training (TR1). They should have made use of the experience of the teachers in the group. (TR5)

The second extract shows how Mamoon has grouped together the data from across his interviews, after coding them. This is his version of undertaking what I have called step 5. You can also locate this in his analysis process by looking at Figure 1, box 12.

Extract 2 from Mamoon's transcript of the topic: Trainees

Category 1: Needs

Q4/N2A: In my opinion, the current INSET concentrates on the general theoretical subjects such as the philosophy goals of the Jordanian

Educational System and it leaves out the practical side and what we need as fine art teachers.

Q5/N2B: INSET must be built on a strong basis. They must consider what teachers need and organize it in a proper way.

Q6/N2C: We found the current INSET programme tried to cover the new curriculum units from the key 4 to key 10, not what we needed.

Q20/N2D: OK, let me ask you about the weaknesses of this programme? Finally, why do I need this kind of training at my age and with my experience after 17 years?

Q21/N2E: I think the tendency of any INSET programme should come from what I need as a teacher, and what I need is the practical skills not just theory.

Q22/N2F: If I was a decision-maker, I would do survey research. This survey would include teachers' opinions and needs. I would do that if I wanted to design INSET that has value in the field.

Q12/N3A: First of all, I would want to know what are the teachers' needs and what are their conditions in their schools.

Q17/N5A: They do not meet teachers' needs.

Q17/N5B: Teachers were not asked about them. Everything followed the opinion of officials in the Ministry of Education Training Centre.

Step 6 Analysis to interpretation

Having gone through the first five steps above there is a final stage of analysis left. In this final analysis stage the data are subject to a refining process. By that I mean the chunks of data under the specific categories are read for different subtleties of meaning. This is where the interpretive process takes over from the descriptive.

Having put together the coded transcripts, the researcher writes a statement that supports the data organized within the categories. These statements summarize the findings within that category as interpreted by the researcher. This is the end of the analysis stage, which now forms the basis for an understanding of what is going on. This material will continue to be worked with to offer a theoretical explanation of the phenomena under study.

Let us look at the stage from analysis to interpretation in more detail by going back to my example given above. The category headings are replaced with statements that indicate the differences as well as the similarities in the teacher perspectives in the various topics: assessment, management, teaching, curriculum etc. These statements give an interpretive summary that is generated by the data. Earlier in this chapter you have seen part of the transcript from one interview and an example of coding for assessment in that transcript. In this research there were six heads of English departments interviewed and so the next stage would be to code all of them with reference to assessment. So given that has been done and all the data have been copied and pasted under the relevant category, the interpretive statement can be written. A short example might help here to illustrate what I mean, using a piece of data from the extract you have seen that I categorized under 'Teacher assessment':

> *D:* I am quite pleased to be in a position where I have to say to people I want to see records, I want to see assessment. I must say I am quite pleased about that because I think it has been a failing in even good English faculties over the years I have been teaching that we depend so much on a teacher's opinion and what a teacher carries around what is in his/her head and when they go unless they write meticulous notes you have lost it all. So I am actually quite keen to have them assessed . . .

With these data, alongside other data from the other interviews that came under the category 'Teacher assessment', I was able to interpret subtleties of meaning with regard to the heads of department's perceptions of teacher assessment among their own departmental members as follows:

> Although HODs have generally seen their role as including having to monitor assessment and record practice in the department, the mandatory nature of the National Curriculum assessment structure has made their job, as a manager of departmental assessment policy and practice, a reality.

The data chunk shown here would be evidence for making this statement, alongside data from other interviews. Of course it would be impossible, unwieldy and a very long read if you included every piece of data to support each statement you made. You would in your research paper or report be selective. For example, in this instance I might use that piece of data but if I wanted to be briefer then I might take a piece of data from another interview to illustrate the point more succinctly. For example:

> Although HODs have generally seen their role as including having to monitor assessment and record practice in the department, the mandatory nature of the National Curriculum assessment structure has made their job, as a manager of departmental assessment policy and practice, a reality. One head of department put it like this:
>
> One of the benefits of Key Stage 3 has been that we now have moderation of pupils' work in the lower school. It has become the framework within which we do it. The need to do that is to me totally beneficial.
> (HOD/AM in interview October 1993)

That might be the only piece on that issue in the research paper, but the rest of the data would be there, in the background as part of your audit trail, your justification for that statement.

The completion of this descriptive/interpretive stage of the analysis would result in your ability to read with clarity and insight the findings of the research investigation under the different topics. However, once you have completed the analysis the real work of interpretation begins. This is when you go on to explore and seek out relationships and patterns, making connections across topics and categories. This leads you to make abstract conceptualizations of the phenomena under study. In this particular project the understanding gleaned through the data analysis indicated the changes that the HODs were going through in the reconstruction of their roles as professional educators having to manage the changes in both the curriculum and their working relationships in their respective departments. Assessment is a key dimension of the work of teachers and it acts as a useful window through which to gain insights into teacher response to change that is externally imposed. Through cross-referencing and relating the assessment data to the other data sets I can go beyond the interpretive and start to theorize. This is a good example of how within interpretive research it is possible to generalize in the sense discussed in Chapter 3. My interpretation led me to conceptualize that the process that teachers are engaged in when accommodating the externally imposed curriculum and assessment changes into their working practices as teachers can be termed pedagogical constraint. I called it pedagogical constraint because the analysis of the six HODs illuminated for me that they have had to make changes to their professional practice in order to achieve outcomes that present a picture of doing the job effectively. At a time of redundancies, economic limitations and external inspections following a particular framework, to be seen to be effective is crucially important. The term pedagogical constraint incorporates centrally the notion of power into the analysis – the power to resist or accept the change. Pedagogical constraint is a micro-political concept, thus enabling the interpretive process to focus on National Curriculum implementation at the level of classroom practice. It indicates the particular ways in which external imposition has been responded to by the teachers and the effect these have had on their approach to decision-making about what to teach and how to teach it. This concept 'pedagogical constraint' was generated by this research and it is more fully described in the published research paper, one of the project outcomes (Radnor *et al.* 1995).

Concluding thoughts

In this chapter the process of analysis and interpretation has been discussed. The chapter focused on a means whereby the interpretive researcher can organize the data for thorough analysis to support her or his interpretation of the situation under study. Although the chapter emphasizes the systematic nature of the procedure, it has to be recognized that a systematic approach does not tell the researcher what the data are saying. It merely helps the researcher to get the most out of his or her data through a thorough exploration of the material from which the researcher will interpret. As the basis of interpretive research is the epistemological position that knowledge is socially constructed and that we are in a world of multiple constructed realities, it has to be the responsibility of each researcher in interrogating his or her data to engage in the creative, constructive intellectual process of making sense of the data and theorizing from it. The challenge is one of illuminating and clarifying the everyday theories that people have that inform their conduct and their response to life experiences.

This move from the analysis structure with its defined stages to the interpretive stage is one that the inexperienced interpretive researcher often finds difficult to make. It feels to the researcher a risky business because he or she has to believe in themselves and believe that they can demonstrate sensitivity towards the data and the ability to bring out the meaning that will both resonate with the research participants and reveal new knowledge to the wider research community. Knowing your data, thinking clearly and believing that authenticity and creativity go hand in hand are key ideas expressed in the final part of this book, to which we now turn. It has been written to help to give the nascent interpretive researcher the courage to make that leap from descriptive analysis to interpretation with confidence and pleasure.

Part 3 | Describing interpretive research

Part 3 contains one chapter in the form of a scripted conversation. The script concentrates on the process of data collection, analysis and interpretation that the researcher is struggling to articulate, describing his journey from a beginning researcher to a more experienced research practitioner. It is a 'tutorial style' conversation that supports the researcher in sorting out his ideas about research in order to write a methodology chapter. The intention of this dialogue is to give a practical example of someone grappling with the key aspects discussed in Part 2. These will surface here as particular practices, questions or dilemmas in this research student's process. Cross-references to the relevant passages in Part 2 are made.

6 | Researching your professional practice

This chapter takes the form of a conversation between myself and one of my PhD students who is carrying out an interpretive research study entitled *Actors' Praxis in a TIE Setting*. As the subject of the conversation is theatre in education, before embarking on the reading of the conversation it would be helpful to understand a little about the nature of TIE. Theatre in education, like all forms of theatre, is a socially oriented activity usually taking place in a defined space and requiring the willing and tacit agreement of all involved to be bound by the conventions necessary to sustain an awareness of fiction (Ben Chaim 1984: Chapter 6). TIE is usually 'bought in' by schools and colleges. It is rarely the case that the audience pays directly. It is provided by the school/college out of its funds. Others (usually teachers) decide who should attend, so rarely does the audience freely choose whether to go or not. The audience is also a captive one, with the event taking place as a timetabled one. Its prime intention is to involve the audience at a physical, emotional and intellectual level to learn something through engagement in a theatrical experience. Central to the work of TIE 'are the twin convictions that human behaviour and institutions are formed through social activity and can therefore be changed, and that audiences, as potential agents of change, should be active participants in their own learning' (Vine 1993: 109).

Reading the conversation

When reading this conversation it would be helpful for you to understand the purpose of the research being discussed. The conversation between the research student and myself as supervisor presents an opportunity for the student to articulate and make explicit the process he is going through, which in turn places the practice of analysis under scrutiny. It also enables the student to rehearse his interpretive propositions; talking about them to others develops his ideas and hunches and opens them up to critical reflection. The research approach advocated in this book emphasizes the inductive nature of interpretive research. The challenge is one of illuminating and clarifying the everyday theories that people have that informs their conduct and their response to life experiences. In engaging in this conversation, the student is discussing the subject of his research to come to an understanding of the meanings embedded, responding to the question, 'How do TIE actors evaluate their practice?' Interviewing actors in theatre in education and interpreting what they mean when they are asked about how they know that what they are doing is working is the essence of this study. James's research question asks the interviewees what signals indicate to them that things are going well and as a result the notion of signals is central to his analysis. The nature and significance of these signals are at the heart of his interpretive explanation of what is happening during the interactions between actors and actors, and actors and audience, during the TIE event. He draws together his findings from the interviews to develop his thesis. The thesis is therefore the outcome of his inductive research. It is through the process that the thesis is created by the researcher, based on the systematic and painstaking process of qualitative data collection and analysis, undertaken taking heed of the principles of researcher practice. Having begun with no hypothesis to prove but a searching open question to answer, it is what he discovers when he probes the minds of his research subjects that guides his thinking through to the interpretive stage. It is the qualitative responses from his interviewees that set up the platform for his discourse, where he places the knowledge he has gained from his respondents alongside knowledge already in the public domain on the subject under study that gives substance to his interpretation. Thus, the student has fulfilled the key requirement for being awarded a PhD. In carrying out his study, the student has persuaded the reader of his thesis that his interpretation is unique, insightful and justifiable, and increases our knowledge and understanding in this particular field of investigation.

To help to understand where the conversation is leading, a 'flavour' of the interpretation he arrived at is presented here. In this way it is possible to glimpse one aspect of the outcome of his research. The purpose of offering this here is that, I hope, you will recognize when you read the conversation the thinking that led to this opening paragraph of his discursive commentary. Eventually, once he has completed his interpretive analysis, he will lay out his conceptualization of what he has discovered.

> I concluded the previous chapter summarising the findings of the research, which included the conclusion that actors working within a TIE context are alert to identifying critical incidents that are defined by one or more signals. These critical incidents which are accorded the greatest value to assessing the TIE process are characterised by

> distinctive signals occurring simultaneously; or rather the effect produced by the synergy of these signals which, when combined 'expand the diameter' (Goff 1980: 107) of the experience and produce a total effect that is greater than the sum of the parts. The reason for the high status given by the TIE actors toward these particular critical incidents is not based on a crude set of quantitative criteria; the critical incidents are not equated with, say, the winning of 'tricks' during a card game. Instead, it is qualitative artistic judgement by the actor – often intuitive, as the data shows – that understands that these moments of synergy, these critical incidents, have the potential to alter the course of the TIE experience toward a richer and deeper aesthetic and educational level.
>
> (Research notes July 2000)

The conversation that follows indicates the stages in the research process leading to the interpretive stage. At certain points, I signpost forthcoming parts of the conversation that can be cross-referenced with Part 2 of this book, which discusses the topics that arise here. In this way you, the reader, can make a connection between the student's discussion of his practice and the explanation of the process as outlined in this book.

Tutorial conversation between James (research student) and Hilary (supervisor)

Signpost: James begins the conversation by talking about the trialling of interviews to generate a semi-structured interview schedule that focused on what he really wanted to ask. Note the resonance with the section in Chapter 4 on semi-structured interviews. The nature of interpretive research is also discussed.

James: What I am taking advantage of at this time is just to go back to the beginning briefly so that you get the whole run of the experience, because I am able to do that now. This is the original proposal and all the sessions I attended on the research methodology course and the initial sort of questions that I was thinking of. I needed to test those out to find exactly what I wanted to do, so I did a pilot and the approach here was about different key words embedded in the questions I was asking and following those through. I have described this approach as a sort of sprats for mackerel and what sort of language the actors used as stuck around those key words and I came up with a variety of useful categories like learning, experience, change, understanding, engaged and involved and I wrote a little piece – a sort of rationale for the word search (looking through the pilot study) but the matters arising . . .

things; I was beginning to be unsatisfied with the initial research questions and this is all retrospective logic, you do realize. This, taken from the write-up of the pilot tells you how I was thinking at the time, the stage I was at. I quote . . .

'Reflecting on the efficacy of the research questions I noted, in the light of these findings, that they were inadequate in scope, especially in addressing the issue which emerged from the data, of artist responsibility and intentionality. How do actors evaluate the processes they share with an audience during performance? This new level on the emergent design coincided with contact with two books which significantly added to my fresh thinking: Carr and Kemmis (1986) *Becoming Critical* and Schön (1991) *The Reflective Practitioner*. The latter study explores notions of reflection on and in action which resonates strongly with the content of each of the interviews. It also connects with much of the drama and theatre in education literature, particularly the analyses of form and content. Carr and Kemmis's book deals with the critical theoretic perspective research paradigm as it might be applied to educational research. *Becoming Critical* includes an exposition of the term praxis-informed committed action (p. 190), a characteristic of the TIE actor and one which makes satisfying re-connections with the responsibility of the artist' (Research notes July 1999).

Hilary: It is not the case, although Carr and Kemmis would have you believe otherwise, that the interpretive paradigm in educational research does not embrace a critical perspective. It certainly does by virtue of recognizing multiple perspectives and taking all of them seriously.

James: You have still got that kind of tension within TIE, whether the approach is more openly interpretive or directly critical, because especially with the need in latter years, say the last ten years. For example, turning to the health authority, to get money from them there is an uneasy tension there, because obviously the health authorities want people to stop smoking, stop having unsafe sex and so on, but companies want to open it up.

Hilary: I think there is a political change too, a change in the culture of the country which the few remaining TIE companies have had to respond to. As a result, when you look at TIE companies they have moved on from having a socialist, Marxist perspective in the political debate to become much more acceptant of living in a capitalized society. They have to come to take into account the rise of things like consumerism and the fact that the whole knowledge base of our culture has changed – postmodernism, relativism, globalization, technology and so on. So interpretivism can operate in such an environment. A thoughtful way of coping with the 'anything goes' philosophy.

James: On that issue, I have been doing a lot of reading recently about postmodernism and so on particularly within the theatre context but one of the things about postmodernism is that it is based on anxiety, it is trying to deny history and it is trying to double guess the future.

Hilary: Yes, because it is all the time trying to create worlds. Could we move on a little now and could you say a little more about this that I noted [reading from his text], 'especially addressing the issue which emerged from the data'. What is interesting, I know it is difficult to answer but how did, for example, the issue of artistry come through? What made you think to yourself, 'Well that is really what I want to look at, although I did not know initially that is what I wanted to look at'?

James: Exactly, yes, exactly.

Hilary: Where has that come from? I have to say that this is what happens with this kind of research all the time, when you start to think about collecting and analysing your data. It is part of the design process.

Signpost: This following extract gives an indication of one thread of James's conceptual context, as discussed under research design in Chapter 3.

James: I can answer that question because I have reflected on that. It all stemmed from when Malcolm Ross was here doing summer schools and he contacted a Polish woman Atlanta Bisman Stock and in August '93 she talked about responsibilities of the artist and it really sort of – at the time I was interested and I thought I will make some notes – and I made some notes and stored them away but these things are seeds and they grow and I am constantly going back to the thoughts that were stimulated from that quite brief talk.

Hilary: So all the time really there is a dialectical relationship between what you are doing in terms of research and the questions you asked when interviewing people? And what's going on in your head when you try to interpret and make sense of what they say and all the time really drawing from our own experience.

James: Well that's right and during the various phases of interviews what I have been conscious of or gradually coming into clearer consciousness is that during the 30/45 minutes many of the respondents have been going through an act of discovery themselves but similarly I have been as well, not necessarily about the interview, the content of the interview, but my own practice as well and so a phrase or response may trigger a memory of something like this lecture back in the 1990s.

Signpost: Principles of researcher practice are touched on here as discussed in Chapter 3.

Hilary: How would you describe the relationship between you as the researcher and the subjects you are researching?

James: I think that is going to be quite the centre of the whole thesis really. It is, again another thing I am returning to, and it has been your positive influence in terms of not just as a supervisor but the idea of symbolic interactionism. It is to do with how we relate as human beings, how an encounter between human beings should be much greater than the sum of its obvious parts.

Hilary: Yes. Of course. I think that relationship is key to this kind of approach in a way, being able to articulate and sense it, it is what I call ethics-in-action. Perhaps we could come back to this later.

Signpost: The conversation returns to the interview schedule, the format of which is semi-structured, with one major question and a series of pick-ups within the style presented in Chapter 4.

James: Yes. Anyway, what the pilot left me with really, was tremendous. I can't recommend it enough times, doing a pilot, just for the mechanics of doing it, it is very muscular, it gets you fit. What it came down to really, an interesting example from one of the transcriptions, is the beginning of an emergent idea of reflection in and on action; the objective and subjective, although I did not know it at the time. I did not have the language to describe it. That was to come.

What I moved on to then was because of my past company which was then called Rent A Role at the Barbican Theatre, Plymouth. I decided it would be useful just to get them altogether and just talk about TIE, just find out a bit more of the language that experienced actors would have because the pilot interviews were with students who weren't experienced. I recorded the whole seminar that I organized but I have not transcribed it all yet and I am poised on whether to do it or not because there could be some useful stuff there. In the first part of the tape, I explained to a group of four actors. 'My task here', I say, 'is to generate data about how a professional team of actors evaluate what is good and what is bad practice. To do this I would like to use this theatre in education programme called POW WOW, performed by the Belgrade Theatre Company 25 years ago; to use their script as a frame of reference.' This is an important feature of this group interview. This company, Rent A Role, is active, doing high quality work, attracting highly professional experienced people. In recent months, if not years, this company has done quite a lot of work in the same age group – which is 6–7-year-olds – as the one the POW WOW programme was written for. The POW WOW programme first saw the light of day as a three hander. In fact and I thought this would be a good script to use because it is very self contained and it has qualities about which are quite self apparent. Also, importantly it is easy to read and TIE scripts traditionally aren't especially as they are active participation programmes. I then go on to say, 'I have got a couple of questions to get things going which is basically, the POW WOW programme is held in high regard, it is an exemplar because it has been published for one thing, so do you agree? Is it a good piece or isn't it?' They started to discuss their thinking about the work/script based on their current experience.

Hilary: So you asked them to read it to see whether they would engage in it?

James: To discover the language they shared to evaluate it . . .

Hilary: . . . and to evaluate it which would give you some insight into . . .?

James: I didn't really know. I was fishing really.

Hilary: Did it give you any insights?

James: What it did, it sharpened my thinking in terms of . . . these actors, are talking about retrospective experience. They are evaluating . . .

Hilary: . . . using their knowledge and the value that they have to give them something that is new to them. So you were hoping to hear their professional thinking about how they would engage in this.

James: Not engage exactly, no. But rather the means by which they judge the efficacy of it. I don't think any of them had seen it, certainly they had not performed in it.

Hilary: Did that give you anything worthwhile?

James: I can't answer that clearly enough, I don't know. All I realized was that they were very articulate and that it filled me with perhaps more confidence in engaging into another phase, leading into the individual interviews.

Hilary: It might be worth getting it transcribed.

James: Yes, I have been thinking of doing that myself, I have done all my own transcriptions.

Hilary: It wouldn't do any harm to get it done.

James: Again I don't know what I am looking for . . .

Hilary: . . . but if it was transcribed, you would have a chance to dwell on it, to see if there was anything there that might link with later findings? It might be just a red herring even . . . but anyway on the level you are talking about, the level of developing your skills as an interpretive researcher, engaging the process of doing, it gave you something, just the experience of doing it?

James: It gave me a bit of a springboard, a bit more confidence really, that I was on the right lines . . .

Hilary: . . . in talking to actors, that they could be reflective? You could go on and interview others, more confident that the data would be rich?

James: Bearing in mind that the pilot was with students who have no professional experience and this lot did have a lot of professional experience and were able to articulate it, filled me with the confidence that I could then move on to interviewing them separately using the same sort of basic research strategy of semi-structured interviews. Which is what I did. And here they are, this represents quite a long period of time. Here are the interviews; this is the first phase of the analysis, the cutting and pasting, finding categories.

Signpost: The supervisor pushes the student to talk more about his principles of researcher practice, particularly the transactional process connected with his interviewees. It highlights some of the skills of interpretive style interviewing.

Hilary: Before we talk about the analysis can we just dwell for a moment on how you went about interviewing, what stance you took as a researcher.

James: As researcher, researching in my own professional field, I have taken a reflective stance throughout. I locate myself within the research question and the nature of the inquiry. I have entered into the inquiry with humility, wanting to create a trustworthy environment with my interviewee and so have taken time to focus the interview schedule which has come down to one question which I pose honestly, not being influenced by my response to it – getting that out of the way, so to speak by reflecting on it myself – really wanting to be told by them. My main interview question was 'during the course of TIE performance when you are working as an actor, what signals are you looking out for to tell you things are going well?' With each interviewee I approached, I would explain the purpose and ask them to talk to me, have a chat with me. This opportunity to have this kind of conversation felt to me as a kind of privilege. I wanted the sense that we were on an equal footing, that they genuinely believed me when I said I wanted to find out their views. When I first asked the research question, quite often there was a long pause before they began. That indicated to me that they hadn't really thought about it and that was quite exciting in a way. As they started to engage and they started to talk, I became aware that they were actually bringing into consciousness stuff that had been there, had been stored away and hadn't been aware that it was there, their realizations, their understandings.

Hilary: It is so fundamental, isn't it? You probably have not thought about it in that way, but as an actor all the time you are interested in the response you get, asking yourself, did that go well?

James: Mm . . . some were very clear. They probably consciously evaluate each time they perform . . .

Hilary: . . . but most of them don't?

James: Usually it is more intuitive.

Hilary: I am looking at this particular interview [indicating the interview transcript in her hand]. The respondent is very full in her response, very descriptive. She is full of interesting information and ideas about why she thinks things go well or not.

James: This just happens to be a good one, very articulate and very clear.

Hilary: She starts talking and then you ask her to expand, saying to her, 'What form does that take?' And then you are saying other useful things to help her open up more, you are asking her to go back to reflect a bit more. You are trying to get her to go a bit deeper and then you are asking her for examples and then again your questions are helping her to unravel more. I think, yes, she is articulate and clear but you are doing a good job as interviewer, encouraging her to explain herself.

James: Yes, I used supportive follow-up questions to probe deeper, to get them to describe in more detail what they were talking about. It seems, based on experience, that most respondents were much more articulate when talking about particular programmes. They spoke in a more interesting and lively way when they were encouraged to recall programmes that were successful. It gave them something concrete to talk about, to reflect on. By suggesting they think of examples seemed to free them up. It was like helping them step into a room they feel comfortable in and so they can start to talk. This particular respondent we are looking at the moment was fantastically articulate. She in fact was the first one I interviewed. The second one is like a contrast, he found it very difficult to articulate.

Hilary: Yeah, he says here, 'nobody asked me that sort of question before' . . .

James: . . . and he really struggled. A lot of references on past experience and he came up with much the same sort of thing.

Signpost: The conversation moves on to the analysis practice. Aspects of the stages outlined in Chapter 5 appear here.

Hilary: Anyway you have some rich data here to analyse. So how did you go about it?

James: What you are looking at [H looking at the transcripts and interviews] here is a sort of map. It is dated 30 May 1997 and I think it represented a desperate desire to find out what the territory was. To lay it out, spread out the transcripts, in a fan of paper. It really did help, and I picked out certain quotes which seem to be key about what actors look out for, which signals they are looking out for each other and things which are going well in the TIE programme. Beginning with the topic of signals I recognized in reading the interviews there were either coming directly to them through others interacting with them, for example, the audience responding to them directly or they were reading the signals that were coming out of the event. In other words they were reading signals off interactions between others, for example, other actors and the audience. So these two topics came from the question. Firstly, putting the data into these topics, it began to fall into a pattern; categories of, well, for example, to quote one of the respondents, 'visible signals'. This is obviously one to do with everyone moving, everyone talking, the kind of silences that take place, attentive listening, watching, eye contact, quite a few made comments about eye contact and then . . .

Hilary: . . . outward signs of reading the audience?

James: . . . then more internal, under the surface sort of stuff. They are no less potent, things to do with how they were responding to the characters, if they were following the story and so on. I even made a note – it happened quite a few times. I was then able to go into another spiral ring and come up with not only some definite categories which fell into groups of direct signals, the indirect signal, but there was stuff about the form and content of the piece, dealing with the structure, story, character and so on and then this is quite significant, responses that I did not know how to categorize, which was to do with this reflective practice thing. So this is where we were two years ago. It represents a lot of hard work.

Hilary: So these interviews gave you actual things in a way that they articulated about things that they saw which made them feel things were going well, or not going well and things that they felt or they 'read' that were under the surface.

James: Yes, the things to do with the structure of the programme . . .

Hilary: . . . and they related in the main to their response to the programme, to what was going on whilst they were performing. And they also gave you some insight into how they were thinking about all this. That is the other level that gave you these categories, coming from their ability to articulate or not . . .

James: . . . some were able to switch it on and others were thinking out loud.

Hilary: Right, OK, that was how you came up with the topics of form and content and reflective practice and categories within these topics.

James: I also used the idea of 'rules of inclusion' for each of the categories which was very focusing, very helpful. They are very simple, simplistic in some senses but they are very useful.

Hilary: Could you say a little bit more about the rules of inclusion?

James: You had to be quite strict with your findings at this point and of course in some cases one is a bit resistant to being rigorous and strict in that way, but again I steeled myself to do it and each of the units of meaning, cut and paste, paragraphs and bits talking about . . . each of these had to apply to a rule to be included in one of the categories. It goes back to your thinking about the boxes. You know what makes you put that chunk of data in that particular box.

Hilary: Give me one example of how you went about doing this.

James: This is a section from one of the interviews and the actor is talking about a production which she had directed I think.

Hilary: And you would put this bit of the interview under a category heading?

James: Yes, this fell into the category headed 'character'.

Hilary: And what you are going to explain, what you call rules of inclusion is your rationale for putting this chunk of data into that category?

James: Yes, it is quite like looking at the sky at night, you constantly see a star, which is brighter than all the others and you are constantly being distracted by that. I guess that perhaps was one of the reasons why the ancient Greeks started to write stories around these apparent shapes. I mean the shape of Hercules in the constellation does not actually look anything like Hercules, but it must have done to them.

This is quoting one of the respondents: 'One of the children's brother or sister is in Harry's – my son's – class and all the brothers and sisters are very kind of . . . "oh are you Harry's mum?" I don't know whether this is a good thing or a bad thing but it is a sort of aura I seem to have – *she laughs* – and importance anyway, and that is quite revealing I think that they have remembered it and that is the way they perceive it. It is not – oh you are the one that came in and did the theatre play that was good – it is sort of stronger than that.'

So although she does not mention the word character she is quite clearly referring to an experience of young people in her son's class who are relating to her, not as a member of the public or even her own son's mum. She is not an ordinary mum that they remember what she did in their school, but remembering her through the character, so it is about signs there, signifiers – what she is remembering is they are looking at the ghost of the character around her, rather than her as an ordinary person. But then later in the interview, she is a bit more specific, there is another quote here. By the way, 'Safe As Houses' is the name of the TIE programme.

'On "Safe As Houses", what was quite revealing was the pictures afterwards. They did this sort of story book some of them, not all the schools but we did different things with different schools. Most of them did pictures and some of them did story books and what was amazing was the detail. Things like my character, a white T-shirt with the blue flower on and the colour of the head band, things in the right place. I thought that was extraordinary actually.'

Now she is referring directly to the character, Natalie, that she is playing but she is referring to the wonderment of how they responded and remembered. That to her was, I think, a tacit awareness of character from children in the first instance and a very explicit awareness of character in the second. The rule for inclusion for that category – character, I will read that out. It is quite simple. The rules are there just to help the process.

TIE actors recognized that if audiences are to willingly involve themselves creatively with the content of the TIE event, then they must be able to relate to and engage with the form the TIE event uses.

It spelt out for me, if you like, my meaning of the concepts 'form and content', which was the topic heading under which the four categories – structure and conventions; character; role; and story – emerged. In this case it is referring to character and those two examples from that interview most definitely obeyed, if you like, or responded to that rule and were therefore included.

Hilary: So your rule of inclusion becomes the statement you say to yourself explicitly when you look at a chunk of data and decide which category under which topic you put it in. It is in fact asking you why are you putting it in there.

James: Mmm, and what is fascinating is when you collated all these bits, units of meaning within the same category and then you read the document labelled character or whatever it is then you go on to another level.

Hilary: Of course you do, because you start to then analyse within the way you have ordered/organized the data. Gathering the data together in this way offers you new perspectives. The focus the category has given you and the juxtaposing of the data of different interviews under the same category gives you the opportunity to reflect deeper on meanings. You begin to see the detail and think about all the nuances.

James: It becomes social again because you are reading more than one person's view.

Hilary: You begin to get a kaleidoscope, a picture.

James: You engage in the specific activity of semi-structured interviews, one to one, and then it opens up into a social universe again when you put the pieces from different interviews together.

Hilary: But this ordering and sorting, if done mechanically, can get you only partly there. This is one of the problems about describing the method and you have done it very systematically and so a quick look at what you might have done, I know that some people's response might be, goodness, you have quantified the units of meaning across the interviews, not realizing that counting them helps you to recognize similarities in response as well as differences in response across your interviews. You balance well between the dialogue which keeps going on in your head between the data and the interpretation, which is happening all the time. All the time you are standing back and looking at it, but you are also thinking about it and trying to make sense of it, but trying to keep it outside yourself by generating categories that you are trying to get the data to match to. It is very difficult, it is also quite complicated to explain to people. To use the term of iteration through analysis and interpretation is easy but to engage in the process of doing it some people find difficult.

James: I found it is a very wearying experience and you have to pace yourself because I did all my own transcriptions because I wanted to feel the data, because it was often the silences which were terribly important as well. One of the things I found useful is to step away from the desk, make a cup of coffee and come back to the data and say, 'What is she saying, what is this really about?' And then you find yourself doing what, I remember reading about what Gramsci did in prison. He used to write heaps and heaps about what was going on outside his cell through the process of discussion in his head. He used to conduct imaginary debates between Lenin and Groce. That was the means whereby he generated his notebooks. This internal debate is what you are doing with the data. You are having a discussion, not with the person that you interviewed but with what they are saying and it is terribly difficult to actually make the distinction. You are dealing with understandings which are often epic because they go beyond, especially when they have declared, 'I haven't really thought about this before. Yes, it must mean that.' You are dealing with very fresh stuff, very exciting. Anyway, I got to this stage.

Hilary: You know, what you are talking about now is the heart of the matter. It is about you trying to come to an understanding of their interpretation of the situation. While they are talking about it, they talk about it and then they go, 'Oh yeah', and then they put an interpretation in and then you put an interpretation on their interpretation, and then you give it back to them and it all becomes such an intersubjective experience. You might find yourself saying, 'What am I doing? What is it all about?' But it is about clarification because it is about the whole being greater than the sum of the parts. It is about putting together all these ideas and coming up with something which helps people to understand what they are doing better, so it is about understanding and depths of understanding more than anything else.

James: I like the way you put that. Yes, in trying to come to an understanding and in having established categories, rules of inclusion, it then moved me to the next phase of interviews which was at the company I have been talking about, GYPT. This is when they changed again, the categories I mean, and the rules of inclusion subtly changed. GYPT were a similar group of people to Rent A Role, very experienced and so on and I went back again to these, the transcriptions of this lot over here [Rent A Role] and I redid those again as well based on the new thinking. The categories began to merge together, they began to . . .

Signpost: Here we discern a move in James's thinking. This takes him into a new phase where interpretation starts to take over from descriptive analysis: see last section of Chapter 5.

Hilary: How did you feel that happening?

James: Well, some of the old categories just did not fit. Let me show you an example, one of the areas I was never really happy with was a category dealing about the space that TIE projects take place in. I was not happy with that. I cannot put it into clear words, it just stuck out like a sore thumb. There was an inconsistency about it. My new respondents, they talked occasionally about similar sort of things but they put it in a slightly different way which made me think about it in a different way. So I was drawn from what they were saying and it just, I suppose, threw a different light on the same subject. What clicked for me is that an old category, one that had been going on way back into the pilot, was the idea of group dynamics. One of the signals is you get a feeling the group is gelling together and that would include yourself and that is a very powerful signal, knowing that positive, creative things are happening. So group dynamics is quite key. It is about how the group is working internally I suppose as well. One of the things that informs that is the context in which you are working which of course is the space. So one of the suggestions I made to myself, and it sort of stuck as I was transcribing and working on these transcriptions, is that perhaps there is a whole group dynamic grouping here. One is dealing with the internal dynamic group and the other is dealing with the context of the external dynamic, things like space, light, air, things of that kind that is informing that. And it is just a useful twinning, I suppose a patterning, putting it together.

Hilary: You had these categories and you started to look at these, the initial categories, and as you looked they started to change?

James: Not all of them.

Hilary: No? but the data in the category, you began to view it differently and the category group broke down and the data regrouped within a new category. So, for example, you have a category in your original analysis scheme called group dynamic and the idea struck you that space links with the group dynamic as opposed to being something that stuck on its own, out of context. That's interesting. It is the way the process should operate. It is the outcome of iterative analysis/interpretation.

James: Another thing I was influenced by was my reading at the time, Glasser and Strauss and what they wrote about the properties of categories. That was quite a significant change within my thinking. My respondents were talking about clear signals like movement and tentative looks or shuffling about and passing notes and so on, negative signals but it is when those movements or when those speech acts became purposeful, it became a property of a category.

Hilary: So the notion of purposefulness starts to creep in and this underpins differences within the category. It is possible now to indicate subtleties of meaning?

James: It is that – so if a child, say, during the course of a TIE programme started to shuffle away from the front of the audience to the side, which sometimes they do for all sorts of reasons, yes, that would be a signal, but if it was to talk to another character that would be purposeful. They move for a reason that was positive within the context of what is being attempted. So the signal wasn't as arbitrary as the interviewee originally thought, what he or she remembered evaluating at the time. They were conscious of signals that they initially responded to ambiguously because they couldn't quite make sense of them but when they looked more carefully it became clearer. It was when it became clear, what it ultimately means that made it a property of a category. So there is a distinction there which needed to be acknowledged. It wasn't just simply a movement.

Hilary: What you are talking about here, is that the actor interprets the actions of the audience and that in itself is what feeds back into the actor interpreting one way or another which will influence their reactions, what they do next as the basis of the TIE programme is participatory.

James: On another issue, another significance if you like, was the comments the actors made about teachers and their responses to what was going on during the action and outside the action. This became a category under the topic heading 'indirect signals' and that was indicative of the way this particular company [GYPT] functioned in contrast to the other company [Rent A Role] who have less contact with teachers. Teachers always had a very, very close contact with GYPT.

Hilary: Mm, they always want to see their work in the context of the education . . .

James: . . . a lot of planning involves teachers before and after the programme as well . . .

Hilary: . . . to make it relevant to what is going on.

James: But what was also beginning to emerge is an overlapping going on, talking about role, character and the structure at the same time. There were overlaps going on. At the time I did not know whether I should worry about it or not.

Hilary: You mean there were overlaps in the sense of . . .?

James: . . . they obeyed more than one rule of inclusion.

Hilary: Well they would – data need not be mutually exclusive, people generally refer to a number of units of meaning in the same flow of speech. What becomes quite interesting is the things that are linked together in their talk. In other words does that linkage happen in the talk of the different people in the study? You start to see connections across certain pathways, your categories. This is the sort of thing that gives you the insight you are looking for.

James: Yes, it was a double edged thing and there was relief in realizing that it was not another separate category.

Hilary: No – this piece of data can be dropped into three boxes.

Signpost: James develops his thinking to the extent of linking his conceptual context with the data, which generates the notion of critical incidents. This becomes important for his thesis.

James: But my anxiety at the time was, should I be concerned about that? Is that significant or isn't it? Not being particularly experienced, I made a mental decision to put that on hold and worry about it later. I invited them to comment on 'the life of the actor' as their commonality and I discovered a commonality. Actors quite often don't work in TIE or other similar kinds of theatre in a purposeless way. They have a purpose, they have got a drive and this probably relates not only to the idea of praxis which is what they are evaluating but the idea of promises which is about the idea of the artist having the desire to start finding truth and morality but it is purposeful, it is not just 'making a chair'. It is more to it than that. It is that which is interesting. Perhaps the desire of promises in this case is more to do with actors who desire to create significant dramatic incidents that are meaningful – the educational aspect, I suppose the sense of morality – in some way rather than just acting. I felt inclined to call these moments critical incidents.

Hilary: What you say is quite interesting. I was recently involved in producing a programme that employed young actors in their first job, which so happened to be a TIE production. So they were not experienced. They were experienced as far as they had a training but this was their chance to launch themselves and basically they were interested in acting. They did not have a concept of TIE as something they wished to do but it gave them the opportunity to perform professionally and two of the three of them also performed in the video production of the play which gave them something which they could take with them for further jobs and so on. They didn't fall into the category of the kind of committed person who wants to use theatre as a means to generate something greater than just their own sense of performing. So acting can operate at different levels. Does your analysis framework take that into account? And are you making a case for the experienced TIE actor behaving in a way that is different from the behaviour in a conventional theatrical performance? Are you getting responses from them that indicate what they evaluate as a sign of things going well as being connected with being in a dynamic role performing something in an interactive way that has an educational context?

James: I think what you just said connects with the idea of purposefulness as it were. It is making the distinction as well. I am paraphrasing of course but there have been descriptions of – during the moment of performance the actors are aware that a member of the audience is moving away from the group and immediately, they could be in the middle of a speech, simultaneously they are thinking, is that child in distress or does it just need to go to the loo or is it acting independently within the fictional context? Is it going to initiate? And all these things are going on and each of those thoughts that quite a few have managed to articulate, fall into separate categories in a way.

Hilary: I think it is quite interesting because it is so different from when you perform in the usual way. Normally, in the theatre context, the audience have chosen to come and know how to behave. These are the rules and the game being an audience watching a play. But in the TIE context and the school context none of that is relevant, there is something else going on about them. This being part of the environment of school but not quite the same as everything else, so quite how do you behave? Did anything come up at all with anything in relation to the notion of control.

James: Control?

Hilary: Just control as an overarching theme, the notion of control coming out of your analysis. This process we talked about where you begin to sense connections between categories. This is how themes emerge.

James: Well one of the things, certainly through interviewing the GYPT people which was challenging to my thinking as well, is that it is one of the things that they don't talk about in a direct way, but they are referring to it as the programme structure, the way it is organized and the drama conventions that are used. They are asking themselves, is it over-controlling, is it constraining the group?

Hilary: And what does that mean and how do you sort that out in a school environment where discipline is expected?

James: Exactly . . .

Hilary: . . . and the nature of lots of different levels of control too, control of their thinking, control of their movement and so on.

James: I would say also that that is a fairly consistent signal that we are on the lookout for, the audience beginning to take control of themselves and beginning to initiate through the level of contributions or moving physically through the space or whatever. There is a wonderful example, it is in the third interview. The theatre piece was about the entrapment like the beast of Bodmin Moor, entrapment of a feral human being who didn't speak, didn't have social language but was clearly human and during the course of that programme which was about language and literacy and so on was for the young people to explore ways of making contact and communicating and so on. This particular respondent refers to this moment when one child who is terribly nervous of the character, a signal in itself, started to move her fingers towards it and the actor noted this and made a conscious decision, 'Shall I not respond? Shall I withdraw or shall I move towards the child as well?' There is this moment when not only did their fingertips started to move together but the whole group focused on that moment. It is just, as the guy said, a tremendous dramatic moment, one that could not be repeated. It is those moments, it is these critical incidents that are stacked up with so many different signals; they converge. It seems that those signals that were most valued were the signals that were combined with other signals.

Hilary: Because that is also about being responsive towards that situation, one of the rules of the 'play in performance in the theatre' is that that doesn't happen, no matter what the audience is doing, they carry on regardless. But within TIE, the responsiveness to the audience in the TIE context makes 'the play' a whole new experience.

James: Magical.

Hilary: You start to break down the boundaries between the different constructions of reality, the real world of the school/classroom and the real world of the play.

James: Terribly upset, this child, about the character. I will probably use this as an example to illustrate the significance of symbolic interactionism. It was a mirror of her own life experience. She was seeing beyond the characters' signing, signifiers, she was looking beyond that into other signifiers. Beyond the play.

Hilary: It became her construction of reality.

James: It became her own life experience. You were saying earlier about how difficult it is to convey that the breaking down of the data into systematic categories is not a mechanical process. I think the role of the researcher is constantly accepting the obvious signifiers through speech, anecdote, use of language and syntax and all the rest of it and looking beyond that. And when you do group these things together from other interviews that is when the obvious signifiers move on to another level. I would say that the most exciting time for me, is when I am looking through the collated categories; here is one, just general local signals – and it is all the respondents, bring them altogether and it is at that point when you feel permitted to add yourself.

Hilary: To interpret – you see them all there, there they are and you look at them and you say what does this all add up to, what does all this mean?

James: And you are adding yourself at that point.

Hilary: Well you are interpreting – you are taking it and you have got together through using systematic analysis, you've got some rich rich data through which to interpret this as opposed to an impression. You get beyond the impression, the surface. I think that it is a very rigorous activity to get to the point where you have got these units of meaning and how you have got them. Once you have got them, you are able to dwell on them and start to interpret from them.

James: Also again going back to the idea of properties within the categories, these are vocal signals, purposeful verbal signals, obviously purposeful vocal signals tend to be in language – and the way it came out, it clarified the rules for inclusion because they were stacked on top of each other, they were related, they clarified each other. I began to feel confident about, yes, this is something that is going to stick now.

Hilary: It holds together. It is robust.

James: Yes, that's right. It's holding.

Hilary: Do you feel confident to use it as a basis to be able to theorize around the data, to come up, perhaps, with concepts that start to give a theoretical representation?

James: The patterns that are emerging is that there are definitely some categories that were more favoured than others. This represents the overlapping thing that I am trying to explore, to see how they were bunching up together, and this forms the basis of my writing so far, which is talking about the findings so far, possible substantive theory emerging to do with the convergence of many categories creating critical incidents of significance. You mentioned themes, how they seemed to emerge out of the analysis? Well one theme that is emerging is the actor as artist and the responsibility of the artist. The analysis of interviews highlights an awareness of best moments when more than one signal is present which I describe as a synergy of different signals coming together; really fizzing, buzzing at particular moments. My interpretation of that is the formation of a critical incident in the fabric of the programme. The actor is aware of that and is in control to influence the occurrence of these critical incidents in very subtle ways. For example, Bodmin Moor when the decision of the actor playing the beast, the intuitive decision of that actor to let the child take his hand – this became a critical incident of significance for the whole group – the whole group had to note and act on it. It was a moment of pure theatre. This was a chance occurrence but I ask the questions: Is it possible for the actor to be more consciously aware of the possibilities? Can the actors create a climate for these things to happen, when the actor says, 'If I do this now, then this might happen?'

Signpost: As his supervisor, I ask James to articulate where he is in the research cycle. I encourage him to think more clearly about the research process, his journey through it and how he will write it up in his thesis. The issue of validity of interpretation discussed in Chapter 3 is raised.

Hilary: So where are you now in the research process? In terms of the interpretive design process it seems to me that you are well into the cycle of analysis/interpretation building up to your presentation of the situation.

James: I am now into the final phase. There are interviews which I have not yet processed. There is one who is a newcomer, not only to TIE but to acting generally. There is another who is an experienced actor. I have the idea that it is a form of triangulation, testing what I perceive to be quite rigorous, to use your phrase, categories. These are people who have done TIE but haven't done it for many years and I want to see what they come up with. Do they talk about the same categories, are there new ones? I am moving towards the idea of theoretical saturation which I need to discover. Interviewing, if you like, a very naive actor has its advantages, tremendously inarticulate, has not got the language to describe it at all, struggled very much at the interview. I think the interview context as well was a problem, very similar to one of my pilot students, who actually struggled with the process of being interviewed. Again I will process it. I know there are one or two things that she does talk about but there is a lot of intuitive stuff.

Hilary: How are you going about analysing it, are you going to use the categories and look for data that fit the categories?

James: Yes that is right, and also to see if there are other categories.

Hilary: And look to see how many occasions the categories . . . you have got your template now of your analysis and you are going to look at this and say, well, where does this fit into this. Then you look at this and you say, well, 'OK I can put that into this but really is what she is saying about something else.' So you are doing two things. You are seeing the match and you are seeing whether it is more than just a match or whether the match is distorting what the interviewee is saying. So that will be quite interesting.

James: I am planning to do three more.

Hilary: And how long are they lasting these?

James: Thirty minutes.

Hilary: Is that long enough?

James: I think so. You sense they tire. For me, the most interesting in-depth responses come about two-thirds in and then towards the final third they start to repeat themselves. Repetition starts, they just start to get bored or distracted. Of course the most challenging is my own and again I am not very confident or clear about how to approach this at the moment. I have got to give it some thought before I seriously look at this. During my last time of GYPT, based on the categories, and these are the old categories I compiled a questionnaire as you can see, and each time I performed as an actor, and it was an all-day programme so there were two occasions and one at half time lunch time and one at the end of the school day, I sat down and reflected on my experience and ticked a category if it was apparent to me, if I was aware that that was going on at the time. In each case, morning and afternoon and some comments as well at the school I went to, so in a way I did what Donald Schön recommends which is that the researcher should go back to his or her own practice. This is my attempt to do that, to put myself, as it were, through an interview of a sort. I am not certain what to do with this.

Hilary: I think it is useful in seeing the things that are meaningful to you and how they link in, in relation to what you are finding, but on the other hand because of your training, now, as a researcher you are affected by that in terms of the level of consciousness of what you are doing. So, really, you are reflecting on the whole reflective process of being yourself. I think it might be probably of most use when you are in the commentary or the discussion stage. I think it will help you to clarify your interpretation of what you have done. It is clearly helpful in discussing your methodology.

James: One of the reasons for doing this is that was I aware of other categories, I suppose. It was not an attempt to self interview myself, it was to test the temperature, to use your phrase. I want to be inside this process myself – curiosity.

Hilary: You've generated an analysis framework and as well as seeing how other individuals fit into it or not, you are interrogating it as well. It is taking it a stage further than often it's taken, because at one level you have probably got enough with what you have done. It is also going to another level of developing the methodology too. You will have something to say about the methodology that enabled you to be confident about your analysis framework. What I mean by this is the writing about the theory of the method you have employed which is different from the theory of what you are finding. This is where you discuss how you came up with your analysis framework. This is where your personal reflections on engaging in the process yourself will be very illuminating.

James: How the methodology is affected by my approach to it, so I ought to refer to the literature in terms of an approach on how to generate the data because of the nature of the interrogation of the data.

Hilary: Yes, but that should clearly be in your methodology chapter. When it comes to discussing what your research is about as opposed to the process of doing the research, it can be done in a more integrated way than is traditionally the way of putting together a thesis. It can be more like a conversation, a conversation about what you find with the findings not separated from the commentary about the findings. Your findings will be able to be presented in the form of themes, key ideas that you want to talk about which will form sections or even whole chapters. These chapters will have in them the data, the analysis and interpretation of the data and the literature that is relevant to that theme. It is much more interesting writing it up like that and more suitable to the interpretive approach if there is a dialectic between analysis and interpretation in your writing. But until you have completed your interpretation and generated a conceptualization of what your research has discovered, it is difficult to decide exactly how put it altogether. You are not yet quite at this stage. You need to finish the analysis stage and complete your interpretation. This conversation has certainly informed me about where you are in your research and importantly has given me insights into your understandings about what you have been doing. So thank you for that.

James: Talking about it in this way has helped me clarify a few things. I feel I have come a long way from that moment I came to ask you if you would take me on as a research student. That was at a time when I had a strongly felt need to positively respond to the changing circumstances in my professional life as an actor, to find a way forward, to understand my professional situation better. I feel I am really doing that now and want to say something about that in my thesis. So just before we finish I would like to read you something I have written that might form part of the methodology chapter. It goes like this.

'Coming to a conceptual understanding of what I have been doing for 25 years of my life has been a liberating experience and what has made it so exciting is the way that the interpretive research process has resonated with my being as artist. When I think to how, when I was engaged as a director at GYPT, we set about devising the theatrical experience it resonates so well with this model of research. Coral Williams's TIE devising model (1993: 98) has four stages: inspiration, gestation, transcription and rehearsal. She says that in the gestation period there are two distinct requirements of actors, research and the creative exploration of the idea. She separates the research activity from the creative process, perceiving the systematic activity of literature searches and locating sources of relevant information as detached from the creative exploration of the idea. But with the experience of interpretive research I believe that research is not just a stage you go through during the devising process but that TIE devising is research. I take a lead from Maykut and Morehouse (1994) when they talk about the qualitative posture taken by interpretive inquirers when conducting research. In Chapter 3 they talk about indwelling:

> To indwell means to exist as an interactive spirit, force or principle-to exist within an activating spirit, force or principle. It literally means to live within . . . being at one with the person's point of view from an empathetic rather than a sympathetic position.
>
> (Maykut and Morehouse 1994: 25)

There are qualities in this language that are the same as that I use in my job as an actor. The devising process naturally aligns itself to qualitative interpretive research as it is an inductive heuristic process which relies on the TIE actor to 'indwell' the tools of theatre creation, to immerse him/herself within the conventions available to the theatre artist to know the social world better. I believe that the process of engagement in the interpretive social inquiry methodology has not only helped me to know what I am doing better as an artist but has built self-confidence in my praxis, in my work as a professional practitioner' (Research notes September 2000).

Endnote

James is nearly at the stage of presenting his thesis for examination. When he came to me to do the research he told me that he was looking for the opportunity to understand his professional situation better. He believes he now does have insights he did not have before and that the ability to articulate what these are has helped him to secure a new direction for his professional practice: a lectureship in community drama in a university college. As human beings we have consciousness. We do things for a purpose. The social world around us is as nothing, for it has no physical presence, if we do not have the means to make sense of it. Researching the interpretive way in educational settings gives us the tools to do that, for it essentially engages us, in a deep sense, in articulating our reflections of practice. By understanding that reality is interpreted experience, and by confronting, through the research process, how we interpret our own lived experience and that of others, we empower ourselves to try to transform aspects of our lives. I started this book by writing that education deals with knowledge and the professional educator is a knowledge worker. All the research students present in this book share the sense that the knowledge they have gained as professionals has been a powerful experience for them. Their educational world, they believe, will never be the same again.

References

Adler, P. and Adler, P. (1994) Observation Techniques, in N. Denzin and Y. Lincoln (eds) *Handbook of Qualitative Research*. London: Sage.

Atkinson, P. and Hammersley, M. (1994) Ethnography and participant observation, in N. Denzin and Y. Lincoln (eds) *Handbook of Qualitative Research*. London: Sage.

Ball, S. (1987) *The Micro-politics of the School: Towards a Theory of School Organisation*. London: Methuen.

Ball, S. (1993) Self-doubt and soft data, in M. Hammersley (ed.) *Educational Research: Current Issues*. London: Chapman.

Bauman, Z. (1978) *Hermeneutics and Social Science*. London: Hutchinson.

Beck, R. N. (1979) *Handbook in Social Philosophy*. New York: Macmillan.

Ben Chaim, D. (1984) *Distance in the Theatre: The Aesthetics of Audience Response*. Ann Arbor, MI: UMI Research Press.

Berger, P. and Luckman, T. (1966) *The Social Construction of Reality*. Harmondsworth: Penguin.

Bernstein, B. (1971) On the classification and framing of educational knowledge, in M. Young (ed.) *Knowledge and Control*. London: Collier-Macmillan.

Bloor, M. (1978) On the reanalysis of observational data: a discussion on the work and use of inductive techniques and respondent validation, *Sociology*, 12(3): 545–52.

Blumer, H. (1962) Society as symbolic interaction, in A. Rose (ed.) *Human Behaviour and Social Processes: An Interactionist Approach*. London: Routledge and Kegan Paul.

Blumer, H. (1971) Sociological implications of the thoughts of George Herbert Mead, in B. R. Cosin, I. R. Dale, G. M. Esland, D. Mackinnon and D. F. Swift (eds) *School and Society*. London: Routledge and Kegan Paul.

Bryman, A. (1988) *Quantity and Quality in Social Science*. London: Unwin Hyman.

Cannell, C. F. and Kahn, R. L. (1968) Interviewing, in G. Lindsay and E. Aronson (eds) *The Handbook of Social Psychology. Volume 2, Research Methods*. New York: Addison-Wesley.

Carr, W. and Kemmis, S. (1986) *Becoming Critical*. London: Falmer Press.

Cohen, L. and Manion, L. (1980) *Research Methods in Education*. London: Routledge.

Denzin, N. K. (1989) *The Research Act*. Englewood Cliffs, NJ: Prentice Hall.
Douglas, J. (1976) *Investigative Social Research*. Beverley Hills, CA: Sage.
Durkheim, E. (1956) *Education and Sociology*. New York: Free Press.
Eisner, E. (1988) *The Art of Educational Evaluation*. Lewis: Falmer Press.
Ely, M. (1991) *Doing Qualitative Research: Circles within Circles*. London: Falmer Press.
Erickson, F. (1990) *Qualitative Methods in Research in Teaching and Learning, Volume 2*. New York: Macmillan.
Gadamer, H. (1976) *Hegel's Dialectic: Five Hermeneutical Studies*. New Haven, CT: Yale University Press.
Gadamer, H. (1989) *Truth and Method*. London: Sheed and Ward.
Geertz, C. (1993) *The Interpretation of Cultures*. London: Fontana Press.
Gelven, M. (1970) *A commentary on Heidegger's Being and Time*. London and New York: Harper & Row.
Giddens, A. (1984) *Constitution of Society*. Cambridge: Polity Press.
Giddens, A. (1990) *The Consequences of Modernity*. Cambridge: Polity Press.
Giddens, A. (1993) *New Rules of Sociological Method*, 2nd edn. Cambridge: Polity Press.
Glaser, B. C. and Strauss, A. T. J. (1967) *The Discovery of Grounded Theory*. Chicago: Atlanta.
Glesne, C. and Peshkin, A. (1992) *Becoming Qualitative Researchers: An Introduction*. White Plains, NY: Longman.
Goff, T. (1980) *Marx and Mead: Contributions to the Sociology of Knowledge*. London: Routledge and Kegan Paul.
Gold, R. (1958) Roles in sociological field observations, *Social Forces*, 36: 217–23.
Hammersley, M. (1992) *What's Wrong with Ethnography? Methodological Explorations*. London: Routledge.
Hammersley, M. and Atkinson, P. (1983) *Ethnography: Principles in Practice*. London: Tavistock.
Hargreaves, D. (1972) *Interpersonal Relations and Education*. London: Routledge and Kegan Paul.
Harré, R. (1983) *Personal Being*. Oxford: Basil Blackwell.
Heidegger, M. (1962) *Being and Time*. New York: Harper & Row.
Hughes, J. (1976) *Sociological Analysis: Methods of Discovery*. London: Hodder & Stoughton.
Maxwell, J. (1996) *Qualitative Research Design*. London: Sage.
Maxwell, J. A. (1992) Understanding and validity in qualitative research, *Harvard Educational Review*, 62: 279–300.
Maykut, P. and Morehouse, R. (1994) *Beginning Qualitative Research*. London: Falmer Press.
Mead, G. H. (1932) *The Philosophy of the Present*. Chicago: University of Chicago Press.
Mead, G. H. (1934) *Mind, Self and Society*. Chicago: University of Chicago Press.
Meigham, R. (1981) *A Sociology of Educating*. London: Holt.
Mishler, E. G. (1990) Validation in inquiry-guided research: the role of exemplars in narrative studies, *Harvard Educational Review*, 60: 415–41.
Morley, D. (1992) *Television Audiences and Cultural Studies*. London: Routledge.

Morris, W. (ed.) (1973) *The American Heritage Dictionary of the English Language*. Boston: Houghton Mifflin.

Peshkin, A. (2000) The nature of interpretation in qualitative research, *Educational Researcher*, 29(9): 5–9.

Polsky, N. (1971) *Hustlers, Beats and Others*. Harmondsworth: Penguin.

Pring, R. (1984) Confidentiality and the right to know, in C. Adelman (ed.) *The Politics and Ethics of Evaluation*. London: Croom Helm, pp. 8–18.

Rabinow, P. and Sullivan, W. M. (1987) The interpretive turn: a second look, in P. Rabinow and W. M. Sullivan (eds) *Interpretive Social Science: A Second Look*. Berkeley: University of California Press.

Radnor, H. (1987) *GCSE: The Impact of the Introduction of GCSE at LEA and School Level*. Slough: NFER.

Radnor, H. (1994) Analysing a qualitative interview, in *Educational Research Monograph Series*. Exeter: School of Education, University of Exeter.

Radnor, H. (1996) *Assessment and Control at Parkview School*. Cresskill: Hampton Press.

Radnor, H. and Ball, S. (1996) *Local Education Authorities: Accountability and Control*. Stoke-on-Trent: Trentham Books.

Radnor, H., Poulson, L. and Turner-Bisset, R. (1995) Assessment and professionalism, *The Curriculum Journal*, 6(3): 325–42.

Resnick, L. (1991) Shared cognition: thinking as social practice, in L. B. Resnick, J. M. Levine and S. D. Teasley (eds) *Perspectives on Socially Shared Cognition*. Washington, DC: American Psychological Association.

Rock, P. (1979) *The Making of Symbolic Interactionism*. London: Macmillan.

Ross, M., Radnor, H., Mitchell, S. and Bierton, C. (1993) *Assessing Achievement in the Arts*. Buckingham: Open University Press.

Schein, E. H. (1985) *Organizational Culture and Leadership*. San Fransisco: Jossey-Bass.

Schön, D. (1991) *The Reflective Practitioner*. Aldershot: Avebury.

Schutz, A. (1954) Concept and theory formation in the social sciences, *Journal of Philosophy*, 51: 257–73.

Seltzer, K. and Bentley, T. (1999) *The Creative Age*. London: Demos.

Smith, D. (1991) Hermeneutic inquiry: the hermeneutic imagination and the pedagogic text, in E. C. Short (ed.) *Forms of Curriculum Inquiry*. Albany, NY: SUNY Press.

Soltis, J. F. (1981) Education and the concept of knowledge, in J. F. Soltis (ed.) *Philosophy and Education*. Chicago: National Society for the Study of Education.

Steier, F. (1991) Introduction, in F. Steier (ed.) *Research and Reflexivity*. London: Sage.

Taylor, C. (1995) *Philosophy and the Human Sciences: Philosophical Papers 2*. Cambridge: Cambridge University Press.

Vine, C. (1993) TIE and the theatre of the oppressed, in T. Jackson (ed.) *Learning through Theatre*. London: Routledge.

Weber, M. ([1947]1964) *The Theory of Social and Economic Organisations*. Oxford: Oxford University Press.

Williams, C. (1993) TIE devising model for pit prop theatre, in T. Jackson (ed.) *Learning through Theatre*. London: Routledge.

Index